D0902780

Florida Gulf Coast University

PHOTO BY VANDAMM

THE LITTLE HUT

BY ANDRE ROUSSIN

ADAPTED BY NANCY MITFORD

DRAMATISTS
PLAY SERVICE
INC.

SOUND EFFECT RECORD

The Play Service can furnish the following sound effect record which may be used in connection with productions of this play. This record sells for $2.95, which price includes packing and shipping.

Ship's siren No. 5198

THE LITTLE HUT was first presented in America by John C. Wilson and H. M. Tennet, Ltd., at the Coronet Theatre, New York City, on October 7, 1953, with the following cast:

(In order of appearance)

HENRY .... Colin Gordon

SUSAN .... Anne Vernon

PHILIP .... Roland Culver

A STRANGER .... John Granger

THE MONKEY .... Ray Gil

Staged by Peter Brook.
Setting and lighting by Oliver Messel.
Costumes supervised by Frank Thompson.

SCENES

The scene—a desert island.

ACT I
Morning.

ACT II
Evening—two weeks later.

ACT III
The following morning.

THE LITTLE HUT

ACT I

A corner of a desert island. There are two huts, one facing the audience at L., *and the other half out of sight, an old mast planted in the ground* C., *and an almost horizontal log or coral seat* D. S. *of mast. Attached to the mast are a clothesline and a mirror. Behind the mast is a ladder which leads to a small platform, on the platform is a phonograph with a cord hanging down. A tree with coconuts is* R. *of mast. A hammock hangs between the mast and tree. Near the log is a pumpkin. Various leaves and plants, including a cactus, are around the stage. A mound is* D. L. *below the hut. There are three hats—Henry's, Philip's and Susan's—on the roof of the hut. Gramophone music is heard as the curtain goes up.*

Henry is sleeping under one of the large leaves downstage R. *Off stage a woman's voice can be heard calling. Bright morning light.*

HENRY. (*From under leaf. Petals come flying out.*) She loves me! She loves me not! She loves me! She loves me not!

SUSAN. (*Off stage.*) Darling, darling! (*Enters.*) Oh, there you are! Didn't you hear me?

HENRY. (*Emerging from leaf.*) I heard screams of darling, yes.

SUSAN. And why not answer?

HENRY. I thought you might have been referring to your husband.

SUSAN. Since it could only be you or Philip, and Philip isn't here. Never mind.

HENRY. Anyway, darling, you must watch darling, you know.

SUSAN. Watch darling, darling? Why?

HENRY. Well, you suddenly let it out last night. Philip and I both answered. I thought he looked a bit startled.

SUSAN. Nonsense. I call everybody darling. I always have. Don't be so nervous, Henry.
HENRY. Not nervous a bit, still we don't want Philip to suspect . . .
SUSAN. I hate that horrid word suspect (*Susan pulls cord and gramophone music stops.*)—makes me feel guilty.
HENRY. I feel guilty all right, but if he ever did find out, I should feel like a murderer.
SUSAN. He won't find out.
HENRY. I hope you're right. Up to now he has been wonderfully dense, I must admit.
SUSAN. No, dear, not dense, logical. Philip's whole character is based upon logic. I am his wife, you are his best friend, best friends don't make love to wives and that's that.
HENRY. Susan—please . . .
SUSAN. There can't be much harm in us all being terribly fond of each other. (*Kiss.*) Can there?
HENRY. The trouble with you, Susan, is that you're amoral.
SUSAN. Really! And who began it all in the first place?
HENRY. I don't remember.
SUSAN. Well, I do. Don't look sad, darling. Penny for your thoughts.
HENRY. Just thinking.
SUSAN. Sad thoughts.
HENRY. Not specially cheerful ones.
SUSAN. You've had enough of this life, you poor old thing.
HENRY. I should jolly well think I have.
SUSAN. You know, you ought to be grateful to destiny as I am. Just think of all those terribly charming people on board, all in their watery graves, poor them, while you and I and Philip are roasting in the sun, sleeping like the dead and eating like horses. Are you admitting that it's an absolute miracle and proof that Fate is on our side?
HENRY. She was certainly on our side during the wreck, but I can't help feeling she's changed sides since.
SUSAN. Such a pity you've no faith. I often wonder what I should do without faith.
HENRY. Faith! You mean you are one mass of blind superstition. Faith, indeed.
SUSAN. Stupid you are. It may interest you to know what I saw

yesterday evening. I saw a huge spider in the hut and all night I dreamt of ladders. I suppose you know what that means?
HENRY. Somebody's going to drop a brick.
SUSAN. It happens to mean that a fortunate decision will be taken.
HENRY. Oh, you!
SUSAN. Such things are all inscribed in the Book of Fate for people who know how to read them. Not for people like you and Philip. Destiny could signal madly, you'd never notice. Take the shipwreck, for instance. Were you prepared for the shipwreck?
HENRY. Of course not.
SUSAN. No? I was.
HENRY. Are you sure?
SUSAN. Quite sure. Midnight struck and a dark woman choked. So naturally I felt pretty worried.
HENRY. Oh, naturally!
SUSAN. But not for long. A few minutes later I was standing under a clock when it struck the quarter, so I knew I'd be all right. I think I can say I'm rather good at reading the Book of Fate. For instance, the night before I met you, I dreamt . . .
HENRY. Now, Susan, don't tell me again that you dreamt of a monkey on a stick, dear, it's very rude.
SUSAN. Oh, you remembered. Yes, I can see his sweet little face now.
HENRY. Which meant ten years of Heaven?
SUSAN. The first six have been Heaven. Do you admit?
HENRY. Quite true, they have. Now you wouldn't like to take one more look into your Book of Fate and see how much longer we've got to be here, on a desert island in evening dress, with nothing to read.
SUSAN. I don't see why you should mind being in evening dress. Now, I really might complain, I only hope Mr. Balmain will never see his lovely dress in this condition.
HENRY. Oh, Susan, you are a good girl—does nothing ever get you down? I do love you. (*Takes Susan's hand and sits on root downstage.*)
SUSAN. I love you too, darling, but you're so terribly spoilt. I suppose that's why I fell in love with you, such a change from Philip who is so perfectly balanced. I must have been attracted by all that temperament.

HENRY. Temperament indeed!
SUSAN. Yes, you're temperamental and pessimistic, Philip is the soul of logic and optimism, and that's why I'm so utterly, blissfully happy between the two of you.
HENRY. Utterly, blissfully happy, are you? Well, it's more than I am. Susan, I'm not going on like this. (*Gets up.*)
SUSAN. Like what?
HENRY. This situation. I can't stand it another day.
SUSAN. But, darling, you must until a ship comes. We can't swim home.
HENRY. I don't mean I can't stand the island. I mean I can't stand the way we're living on the island.
SUSAN. What way?
HENRY. What way? I love you, Susan, I've been your lover for six years and now for twenty-three days you've shared the big hut with Philip while I've been alone in the little one. After six years as your lover what have I become now? An old family friend with a cottage in the park. I tell you, I won't put up with it any longer.
SUSAN. Is that why you've been looking so awfully sad?
HENRY. Yes. I've begun to have quite enough. (*Moves to her.*)
SUSAN. But, darling . . .
HENRY. Enough of being with you all day and saying good night nicely when you and Philip—(*Pauses, looks at hut.*) go home together.
SUSAN. But what's to be done about it?
HENRY. I can't understand your attitude, Susan. Don't you ever long to be with me in my hut?
SUSAN. Yes, of course I do. I long for it feverishly—only I never think about it.
HENRY. (*Moves away.*) Yes, well, there you are—I do think about it.
SUSAN. But since there's nothing to be done?
HENRY. I'm going to do something—tell Philip.
SUSAN. Tell him what?
HENRY. Everything. That for the last six years we've been lovers.
SUSAN. You're going mad!
HENRY. Then I shall appeal to his famous logic and optimism and suggest that as we have been sharing you for the last six years, with splendid results for all, nothing would be changed if we go on sharing you here just the same. Nicer in fact for Philip, as he'll

no longer be deceived—that is logic itself—a husband who knows is not a deceived husband any more.
SUSAN. I never heard of anything so cynical.
HENRY. I'm sorry, but just explain what's wrong?
SUSAN. I think it's awful. But you can't be serious, Henry?
HENRY. Oh, yes, I am. I'm afraid it's all written in your Book of Fate, and nothing's to be done about it. Destiny didn't mean me to go on like this. Didn't you dream about ladders? I told you somebody's going to drop a brick. Well, that somebody's going to be me.
SUSAN. Very well, I shall be furious.
HENRY. Who with?
SUSAN. Just furious all round.
HENRY. In my view it's the only normal solution for people in our circumstances. I would even say the only moral solution.
SUSAN. Moral!
HENRY. Yes, moral. I think it's unworthy of us to go on concealing this affair from Philip and I think he'll be most grateful to me for opening his eyes. I'm sure if he were in my place he would think exactly as I do.
SUSAN. If he were in your place he would be my lover, not my husband, but as it happens that he is my husband, I don't somehow think he'll jump for joy when he hears the news. Naturally you know best.
HENRY. Philip is my greatest friend, I know him inside out and I'm perfectly sure he would wish to be told.
SUSAN. Henry, you're not really going to tell him?
HENRY. Yes, I am.
SUSAN. And ask him to share me with you?
HENRY. Yes.
SUSAN. But everybody would say it was total madness.
HENRY. At home everybody would, yes, but desert islands and rafts and things have their own special rules. So, Susan, do you agree?
SUSAN. I don't know. It takes a man to have an idea like that. However. Philip is a man too, so you must simply work it out between you.
HENRY. Splendid. (*Takes Susan in his arms, kisses her.*) Where is he, anyway? Fishing?
SUSAN. No, he's hunting butterflies, I think. Darling . . . um

. . . (*Indicates hammock. Henry comes down and takes down the hammock. Susan collects bag and clothes brush and brushes dress.*) He generally fishes later in the day.

HENRY. (*Undoing bottom of hammock.*) His talent for fishing has certainly proved very useful.

SUSAN. So has your talent for finding truffles, Henry. I think you are both wonderful.

HENRY. (*Goes to top of hammock and unlocks it.*) All the same, I find it odd that such a first-class fisherman, when it comes to huntin' should only care for huntin' butterflies.

SUSAN. He loves butterflies.

HENRY. He never stops killing them.

SUSAN. (*Brushes skirt.*) That's true—that's what men are like, darling. You love foxes, Philip loves butterflies, Spaniards love bulls—it's all the same story, kill, kill, kill.

HENRY. Yes, but butterflies . . . odd somehow. (*Below but with hammock, pulls it down.*)

SUSAN. (*Henry goes up ladder.*) I'm all for it—keeps his tummy down. Bend—stretch—out in the open air. So good for him. That's why I let him have this hole in my stole for a net.

HENRY. What's the time?

SUSAN. Stupid you are.

HENRY. Oh, I keep forgetting. Not bad, living without a clock.

SUSAN. I love it. (*Crosses to hut, puts in bag and clothes brush.*) One less reason for crossness. I'm never late. (*Philip can be heard "hullooing" off stage. Henry comes down the ladder, to Susan's* R.) Here comes Philip—it must be nearly coconut time. (*They both go to tree and shake it until three nuts have come down. Henry catches them and gives them to Susan.*)

HENRY. Well, after coconut time, leave us alone for a bit. What ever you do, leave us alone.

SUSAN. (*Going to hut with nuts.*) I certainly will. Henry, you're not really going to ask him that?

HENRY. I am.

SUSAN. Then perhaps I'll go and have a swim, come back later and pretend it's the first time I've heard of it.

HENRY. Why?

SUSAN. Seems more natural somehow.

PHILIP. (*Off stage.*) OO-OOoo!

SUSAN. Come on, darling, we waited coconut for you.

HENRY. Susan, do you love me?
SUSAN. Of course I do. (*She enters hut.*)
HENRY. You'll see how everything will be all right. Remember the ladders.
SUSAN. (*Her head out of the hut opening.*) Mmm, a pity about the salt, though.
HENRY. What salt?
SUSAN. That Philip spilt at luncheon.
HENRY. Why?
SUSAN. If salt be spilt all the signs are reversed. (*She pulls into hut again.*)
HENRY. (*His face in his hands, stamps.*) You and your signs! (*Philip enters. He is dressed in a dress shirt, coat over one arm, one foot bare and the other in a patent-leather shoe, carrying a curious butterfly net and a basket with butterflies in it. He comes towards the hut door.*) Hello, Philip!
PHILIP. Hullo, old boy! Hullo, darling! (*Susan enters from the hut, kisses him, takes coat, net and hat.*)
SUSAN. Hello, darling, how are you?
PHILIP. I'm dying of heat, and I've brought back a blister.
SUSAN. Oh, poor you. Is that all you've brought back?
PHILIP. Don't laugh. It's exceedingly painful. My foot's practically off. I wish it was.
SUSAN. Oh, poor you. (*She puts coat on cactus and net against hut.*) Why don't you leave off shoes altogether and get used to bare feet? They'll soon harden, like at the seaside when one was little. (*Exits into hut.*)
PHILIP. (*Goes to log, puts basket down.*) I think she's right. Nothing could hurt more than my present blister. I'll give you my left shoe, Henry.
HENRY. (*Comes to Philip, takes shoe to put it on.*) Thank you very much, I shall be glad of it. I'm tired of hopping. But what about you?
PHILIP. I shan't walk so much. (*Takes butterflies out of basket and puts them on log.*) Anyway shoes are one of the things that can't be very well shared like toothbrushes and wives. I'm ready for my nut, darling. (*Henry reacts in the middle of putting the shoe on.*)
SUSAN. (*From inside the hut.*) Coming.
HENRY. Good day? (*Sits below mast to put the shoe on.*)

PHILIP. (*Puts basket under leaf and gets out cork with butterflies on it.*) Wretched. You know that cymophanous skewball I was after?
HENRY. What?
PHILIP. Oh, never mind—your ignorance on the subject of butterflies never ceases to amaze me. The brute got away again. (*Gets cork from under leaf.*)
HENRY. Bad luck.
PHILIP. Wasn't it? It's partly my heel. (*Crosses to log, limping.*) I may do better when my feet have hardened. What are you laughing at?
HENRY. It seems funny, somehow, an old share-pusher like you, getting so het up over a butterfly.
PHILIP. (*Sitting.*) Does it?
SUSAN. (*Entering from hut with three half coconuts on a leaf tray.*) What's the joke?
HENRY. The black-coated worker is in a rage. He's muffed his butterfly.
SUSAN. (*Gives Henry drink.*) Isn't he a blessing? You couldn't say he wouldn't hurt a fly though, could you? (*Offers nut to Philip, who takes it.*)
PHILIP. I don't hurt them, you know.
SUSAN. 'Course not, darling, you kill them with kindness.
PHILIP. All the same I wish I'd got my cyanide bottle with me.
SUSAN. Hope you like it. I put in a dash of eucalyptus today.
PHILIP. That's very daring of you, dear.
HENRY. Well, here we are. (*They drink.*)
SUSAN. And here we stay!
PHILIP. Wonderful drink, coconut. I wonder what will happen if I apply it to my blister? (*Puts milk on heel.*)
SUSAN. What?
PHILIP. It's a pure product, may do good, can't do harm. Here goes.
SUSAN. Let me see. That's the heaven of this place. (*Goes to Philip, kneels, rubs his foot.*) One tries everything. Sooner or later we shall make a startling discovery—like potatoes and coffee. After all, they were found quite by accident, I suppose. Darling, you're very hot. (*Goes to cactus for coat.*) Put on your coat.
PHILIP. All the more reason for not putting my coat on.

SUSAN. (*Puts coat round Philip's shoulders.*) But it's when you're very hot at the seaside that you catch a chill.
PHILIP. Fuss, fuss, fuss. (*Henry signs to Susan to leave them alone.*)
SUSAN. Well, now you're both here together. I'm going for a swim.
PHILIP. Darling, what do you mean, now we're together?
SUSAN. Well, you know I haven't got a bathing suit. If you're both together, happily chatting, I shall feel safe.
PHILIP. (*Kneels to put his coat on.*) What is this sudden access of modesty? Do you expect us to run after you and peep from behind a tree?
SUSAN. Good-bye for the present. (*Starts to leave.*)
PHILIP. Well, hurry back. I won't go fishing till you get back.
SUSAN. Very well.
PHILIP. Don't get drowned.
SUSAN. Stupid you are. I was born under the sign of the Dolphin and it saved me once in a shipwreck. (*She exits.*)
PHILIP. (*Rising.*) I thought you were saved by a floating grand piano. (*Moves to log, sits and puts butterflies onto the cork.*) She swims like a fish, I don't worry about that, but I do sometimes wonder if we are the only people on the island. I must have walked five miles today in the forest. It's not so small as we thought. There might easily be tribes living there.
HENRY. No, I don't think so.
PHILIP. Why don't you?
HENRY. Not very likely. In twenty-three days we'd be bound to have seen signs of them. Do you realize I made the twenty-third notch on the mast today?
PHILIP. Did you really? Over three weeks! Well, I must say it's surprising how quickly one can get accustomed to a primitive life and even enjoy it. The human animal is wonderfully adaptable.
HENRY. You think so?
PHILIP. Of course Susan's had a lot to do with it, treating the whole thing as an enormous joke. Good gracious, I've got that one already—how maddening. Never mind, it'll do for a swap. I always knew I was lucky with Susan, but never realized quite how lucky. All the same, it is a surprise to find oneself happier and more contented every day that goes by, isn't it?
HENRY. Yes, well, things aren't quite the same for me, Philip.

PHILIP. Not the same?
HENRY. I'm not in your shoes, old boy.
PHILIP. But I've just given you my shoes, old boy.
HENRY. (*Goes to mast, puts nut under leaf.*) Very well then, I'm in your shoes, but I'm not in your situation.
PHILIP. What's the difference?
HENRY. You've just said yourself, Susan has a lot to do with it, and that's the point. Susan is your wife, I live alone.
PHILIP. (*Turns to Henry, puts nut in front of log.*) Good gracious, my dear old boy, I'd never thought of that. (*Puts butterfly on leaf.*) I shall have a word with Susan—you mustn't feel left out—though I never think Susan does make very much difference between us.
HENRY. (*Moves to Philip.*) None whatever; Susan is angelic.
PHILIP. Isn't she?
HENRY. A perfect darling. Don't think I'm being reproachful, Philip.
PHILIP. (*Picks up nut, sits on log and drinks.*) You were quite right to mention it, old boy. That's just the sort of thing that makes for trouble on a desert island.
HENRY. No. You don't understand. What I mean is this: I live alone in my hut. You have a wife, you have her near you, a warm, breathing wife, in your hut, while I—— (*Philip looks at Henry.*) You understand, Philip?
PHILIP. Yes, yes, of course.
HENRY. It's like that.
PHILIP. Mm. (*Pause. Suddenly he looks at his foot.*) I say!
HENRY. What?
PHILIP. My blister's come to a head. Must be the coconut. Nature's lasto-plast. How interesting—do look.
HENRY. Very nice.
PHILIP. Isn't it wonderful? It doesn't hurt any more, and it's come to this wonderful head. Do show a little enthusiasm.
HENRY. (*Looks at blister.*) No, no, I'm simply delighted. That'll be something to take home.
PHILIP. Won't it? Coco-plast, the wonderful new remedy, discovered by a shipwrecked financier. (*Pause.*) So, by and large, you are tired of being a bachelor. I knew this would happen. Haven't I always told you that the only real happiness for a man is in marriage?

HENRY. That's not the point.
PHILIP. Yes, it is, old boy. You want someone warm and breathing in your hut. In other words, you want a wife.
HENRY. Certainly not. Never, for a single moment, have I wanted a wife.
PHILIP. Oh, I know a bachelor is a polygamist really. I've nothing against polygamy. Why, half the world practices it. Great tracts of the Orient—Sultans, Pharaohs of ancient Egypt—I'm sure it's quite natural.
HENRY. Yes. Natural for me. And it's natural for women too.
PHILIP. Natural for women, old boy? Oh, no, certainly not.
HENRY. (*To Philip, bending over.*) In the Toureg tribe each woman has many husbands. They are called the People of the Veil.
PHILIP. They may be. All I say is, it's not natural for women.
HENRY. Why not?
PHILIP. Women are never in love with several different men at the same time.
HENRY. Neither are Sultans (*Crouches down.*) in love with several different women. They have one favorite and the others hang about, in case.
PHILIP. My dear old boy, a respectable woman doesn't keep a crowd of men in her drawing room hanging about, in case.
HENRY. Respectable women often have lovers, old boy!
PHILIP. Do you mean married women?
HENRY. Respectable married women. We know several who have lovers.
PHILIP. Do we? Who do we know?
HENRY. Well, what about Dottie?
PHILIP. Has she got a lover?
HENRY. Yes, she went to Paris with him at Easter.
PHILIP. She told me she was going in a party of eight.
HENRY. Yes, well the other six dropped out. The point is, women are polygamous, aren't they?
PHILIP. I can't get over Dottie. For a while, perhaps they are.
HENRY. For a while?
PHILIP. Until they've got their divorce.
HENRY. (*Rises.*) I wasn't talking about divorce.
PHILIP. My dear old boy, (*Henry turns to him.*) a respectable married woman with a lover is a contradiction in terms. Look at it logically. If she's married and respectable she has no lover. If

she's married and has a lover she's not respectable. A little adventure—well, I suppose it might happen to anybody, but I don't call that having a lover. Take it that she tells her husband and gets a divorce, then she is respectable, but she's no longer married. Finally she marries the lover and she's once more a respectable married woman but she has no lover. I think that's pretty irrefutable.

HENRY. (*Sits on log next to Philip.*) One more hypothesis. Suppose she tells her husband about the lover and her husband doesn't divorce her. He likes being married to her. She is always very sweet to him, and he decides to keep her in spite of the lover. Is she not a respectable married woman—with a lover? (*Pause.*)

PHILIP. She's a very lucky woman—yes, I suppose she is.

HENRY. There it is. She has two men in her life.

PHILIP. Mmm.

HENRY. Come now, my dear old boy, we both know cases like that, don't we?

PHILIP. I suppose we do.

HENRY. Now will you agree that polygamy is no more unnatural for women than for men?

PHILIP. Oh, you'd argue the hind legs off a donkey. But why are we talking about polygamy like this?

HENRY. Apropos of my being a bachelor.

PHILIP. Oh, yes, of course. Alone in your hut. And now you see how right I was about marriage. (*Pats Henry's shoulder.*) Poor old Henry—I'm very sorry for you, I feel for you, I feel for you, really I do, and if I could help in any way I'd be only too glad. But the fact is there's nothing to be done, there are no women here, not in this part of the island. Of course if you explored a bit you might find the other end full of People of the Veil who might be of use to you. (*He stands up.*) Good hunting. (*Puts nut in front of log.*)

HENRY. (*Rises.*) Very well, then, since you're so dense I must take the bull by the horns. Philip, sit down.

PHILIP. (*Now turns and looks at Henry.*) But I've just stood up.

HENRY. Yes. I'm asking you to sit down again for a minute.

PHILIP. Oh, very well, if you make a point of it. (*Sits on log facing Henry.*)

HENRY. Philip. We're each other's best friends, aren't we?

PHILIP. Yes.

HENRY. And you know how philosophical you are—always seeing things practically, in the light of reason?
PHILIP. I hope so.
HENRY. Yes, you pride yourself on it, and rightly too. Rightly too —(*Pause.*) rightly too. (*Pause.*) Now, practically and reasonably speaking—(*Pause.*) there's only one way out of—there's only —— (*Pats Philip's shoulder and moves away, saying.*) There's only one way out of our dilemma! (*Turns and comes closer to Philip.*) We must share Susan. (*Philip does not answer.*) Well?
PHILIP. Well what?
HENRY. Did you hear me?
PHILIP. I don't think I heard quite right.
HENRY. We must share Susan.
PHILIP. Henry, don't talk such rubbish. I might get cross.
HENRY. It's the only way I can see out of the dilemma. (*Backs away.*)
PHILIP. I wish you wouldn't go on talking about *our* dilemma. It's *your* dilemma, and nobody's fault but your own, your own silly fault for not taking my advice and finding yourself a nice . . .
HENRY. (*Comes forward a pace.*) Steady, Philip. You've just admitted yourself that polygamy is quite natural, for men and for women.
PHILIP. Is this a dream, or did I really hear your voice asking me to give you . . . ?
HENRY. Susan. Yes.
PHILIP. Is this why you asked me to sit down? I wonder you didn't ask me to lie down. Do you seriously expect me to give you my wife?
HENRY. Not to give. My idea is that we might consider her as *our* wife.
PHILIP. (*Rises and faces Henry in front of log.*) You've said it again! You keep on saying and repeating it! I couldn't have believed it of you, Henry, but I am beginning to see how little I know you. You're a cad, my dear Henry, I'm afraid. Let that pass. There is just one other thing, however—take it that I am prepared to listen to your curious suggestion, there is somebody else to be considered, you know. Susan—is she to be offered up as a human sacrifice? Since we are being so logical, one would have thought that logically the first person to ask would be Susan. (*Henry starts, as if to speak.*) We can soon remedy that. Susan! Susan!

HENRY. I have asked Susan, and she's all for it.
PHILIP. What!
HENRY. I should have told you so at the beginning, but I got involved . . .
PHILIP. You say Susan agrees?
HENRY. Yes, Philip, there's something else I must tell you. For the last six years I have been Susan's lover.
PHILIP. Her lover?
HENRY. Yes, Philip.
PHILIP. Any family?
HENRY. No, no, that's all. You know the whole truth now.
PHILIP. Truth . . . !
HENRY. Yes, Philip.
PHILIP. You've been my wife's lover for six years?
HENRY. Yes. (*Pause.*)
PHILIP. (*Laughs.*) Well, really, you must tell that to somebody else. It's really rather funny. (*Bursts out laughing.*)
HENRY. I don't know what you're laughing at, it's an absolute fact.
PHILIP. My dear old boy, I'm not quite half-witted, you know. Susan and I are famous for being a happily married couple. We are never apart, the two of us—well, the three of us really, we generally do things all three together. There may have been a little gossip but that's unimportant. I know what Susan has been to me, so don't come telling me that my wife's been your mistress because I don't believe it, and, what's more, I don't like it. I know you only meant it as a joke, and usually I love your jokes but frankly I found this one a little on the silly side. And now if you'll excuse me, I'll go and meet Susan.
HENRY. And if I say it again?
PHILIP. Henry, I don't like it.
HENRY. (*Taking a step nearer to Philip.*) And if Susan agrees?
PHILIP. Is this a conspiracy?
HENRY. And if I give you my word of honor?
PHILIP. Your word of honor?
HENRY. (*Holds out his hand.*) I give it. (*They shake hands.*)
PHILIP. Susan's lover . . . Henry?
HENRY. (*Pulls hand away.*) Well, there's nobody else that it could be, is there? Why d'you think I came on this cruise?
PHILIP. Because you said you wanted a holiday.

HENRY. No, no, no, because you'd set your heart on it, and I didn't want to be separated from Susan for weeks and weeks.
PHILIP. Susan's lover . . . Henry!
HENRY. And the only man in the world I would cut myself in pieces for is you, Philip. You know that.
PHILIP. (*Persuaded of the truth at last.*) Well, I'm . . .
HENRY. And you never suspected, did you? We'd have done anything to stop you finding out, our one idea was that you should be happy. Because we love you, old man! (*Philip sits down on pumpkin.*) If I've given you a bit of a shock blurting out the truth rather suddenly, you must remember it's better to learn these things suddenly, it hurts much less than finding out by degrees. Now, as soon as you feel able to give your mind to it, your logical mind, Philip, you will be forced to admit that the situation is unchanged. You've been perfectly happy for the last six years, and we only want you to go on being happy for ever. I haven't upset you, have I, old man? Are you minding very much, Philip? Are you minding very much, old boy? (*Bends over him.*)
PHILIP. I haven't the slightest idea. I wonder I can speak to you at all, but you see I can, and in my ordinary voice. It's very odd.
HENRY. There! (*Pats Philip's back.*)
PHILIP. I feel as if I'd had chloroform, or been under heavy water. (*Henry helps Philip to his feet.*)
HENRY. Yes, well, you've had a bit of a shock, you know. I think you'd better walk gently up and down. (*Puts Philip's arm through his.*) Walk up and down and think of nothing but walking up and down. (*Faces Philip.*) Now just relax. Breathe deeply in through the nose, out through the mouth. Splendid. (*Keeps on the move. Henry breathes three times. Philip starts on the third time.*) In—out—in—out. That's it. Keep breathing, old boy. How's the heel? (*Pause. Looks at Philip.*)
PHILIP. Oh, my heel. Better, if anything.
HENRY. Go on breathing. Don't swallow your tongue, will you?
PHILIP. My tongue's all right.
HENRY. (*Guiding Philip to the log.*) Can I get you a drink? Would you like to have your shoes back?
PHILIP. No, thank you. I'm all right now. (*Sits down on log.*)
HENRY. (*Facing Philip, bending down a little.*) Yes, you're a better color. All the same, you must take it easy.
SUSAN. (*Off stage.*) Hill-oo!

PHILIP. That's Susan. Did you say she knew about this conversation we've had?
HENRY. Yes, we discussed the whole thing.
PHILIP. And she liked the idea?
HENRY. She rather wondered how you'd take it. I think she was afraid you might not understand.
PHILIP. I may not be very quick-witted, but I understand all right.
SUSAN. (*Susan enters with two flowers.*) You must be mad not to go in. The water's never been so wonderful. I swam and swam. (*Crosses to hut and puts flower above doorway.*) Anything the matter? You both look so sad. How's the blister?
HENRY. Philip knows everything.
SUSAN. Indeed he does, he's a walking encyclopedia, the angel. (*Puts a flower onto hut.*)
HENRY. Everything about us, I mean.
SUSAN. (*Turns to Henry.*) Such as what?
HENRY. He also knows that you know that I was going to tell him everything.
SUSAN. All right, I'd better stop looking detached then. Well, darling? (*Stoops to look at Philip, then kneels.*)
PHILIP. Well?
SUSAN. Bit surprised?
PHILIP. A bit.
SUSAN. Don't let it upset you, darling.
PHILIP. No, naturally not.
SUSAN. You must admit we've been rather wonderful all these years, the way we never let you have an inkling.
PHILIP. Wonderful.
SUSAN. Even now I didn't want to tell you, but Henry explained that somebody as philosophical as you are would see at once that there's no difference between the way we've been living all this time and the way we propose to live from now on.
PHILIP. Susan, you've been deceiving me for six whole years.
SUSAN. In a way . . .
PHILIP. I couldn't have believed it of you, I couldn't.
SUSAN. Please don't be sad; now look on the bright side. Think of all the times I've deceived Henry with you, for example. (*Rises. Susan and Henry look at each other.*)
PHILIP. Indeed?

SUSAN. Over and over again; I feel ashamed whenever I think of it.
PHILIP. Don't torture yourself, I beg.
SUSAN. The times I've put him off for dinner with a plain lie, saying one or other of us had a headache simply because I wanted to spend the evening alone with you. Remember, I did it just before we came away, and by nine we were happily in bed with a book.
PHILIP. I've noticed that as a rule whenever you're in bed by nine, it's because you want to finish a book.
SUSAN. (*Sits on log next to Philip.*) Yes, dear, to finish a book, blissfully lying by your side, darling. Such nice evenings we used to have, with me screaming at the jokes every now and then. Do you remember how I used to put my head on your shoulder (*Puts her head on his shoulder.*) so that we could both read together, and gradually the noise of the traffic would die away, and later on perhaps we'd hear that owl in the park? Happy life we've had, really. Of course, dear, you couldn't know what I did, that poor Henry was pacing up and down somewhere, eating out his heart with jealousy, or trying to forget, all alone at the cinema. He had nobody at home reading a book in his bed. And that's something I've never done with Henry—I've never looked at a book when I've been in bed with Henry. (*Philip looks at Henry.*) Do you know, we've never been alone together very much, just sometimes in the afternoons when you were at the office. (*Philip looks at Susan.*) And then you always got back sharp at six, and you never went there *at all* on Saturdays and Sundays. Henry and I might have loved to go off at week-ends together sometimes, but no! (*Strokes his face, he looks ahead.*) The week-ends were consecrated to you. We've never been for a journey together. Yes, once, that time you were in Liverpool, on business. (*Philip looks at Susan again.*) And how it poured, and I was in agonies lest you should find out, and it wasn't cosy a bit. So you see, poor darling Henry (*Rises.*) has never had a few cosy days with me in his life. You've always been there to stop it.
PHILIP. I plainly see I've been nothing but a kill-joy.
SUSAN. (*Crosses to mast.*) Stupid you are, Philip. You're simply trying to hurt our feelings. (*Below foot of mast, looks at Henry.*) There were times when we used to say wouldn't it be lovely if we could do this or that, if only Philip weren't there we could, but of course he is there, the darling, so we can't. You see? We never

felt you were in the way the very least little bit; we just took you for granted. I do wish you would cheer up. You seem to forget that I am your wife, and Henry—Henry (*Holds out her hand to Henry, who takes it, coming to her side.*) is your best friend.
PHILIP. Oh, no, I don't.
SUSAN. Then why are you so gloomy? (*Henry drops Susan's hand. Susan looks at him.*) I do think men are peculiar. I challenge you to quote one single instance in the whole of our married life when I haven't been a perfect wife to you.
PHILIP. But my dear child, you've just said yourself that you've been unfaithful to me for years.
SUSAN. But I've been unfaithful to Henry, with you for years, so that must cancel out. (*She stoops by the side of him.*)
PHILIP. (*Giving it up as a bad job.*) Oh, well, it's all in the past now.
SUSAN. Exactly! (*Puts her arm round him, kneeling.*) All over.
PHILIP. Is it?
SUSAN. I mean keeping it a secret from you is all over, and you'll never be able to say, in future, that we're deceiving you, will he, Henry? You can't deceive people when they know.
HENRY. Do stop baiting poor Philip.
SUSAN. I'm not baiting him, am I, Philip? I'm clarifying the situation.
HENRY. Yes, well, it's perfectly clear already. I think Philip would like to be left alone for a bit. Wouldn't you?
SUSAN. Would you?
PHILIP. No, thank you.
SUSAN. (*To Henry.*) There, you see, my darling?
PHILIP. See what?
SUSAN. I was talking to Henry.
PHILIP. Oh, he's darling now, is he?
SUSAN. It's more natural, as you know everything. But not if you don't like it though, Philip.
PHILIP. No, no—I must simply get used to it—like walking barefoot and (*Looks at Henry, Henry steps back one pace.*) everything else.
SUSAN. (*Rises.*) I generally call you darling, and Henry my darling—it's just a habit—and here it might be more convenient.
PHILIP. All right. How's it going to be arranged?
SUSAN. What do you mean?

PHILIP. I know the worst—I've swallowed the pill. What are the plans?
HENRY. The plans?
PHILIP. The *modus vivendi*, if you like.
HENRY. Just—go on as we were.
PHILIP. I don't go to the office here.
SUSAN. Darling, what's all this about? Nothing's changed in any way, we keep on telling you so.
PHILIP. I don't want to dot the i's and cross the t's but well—of course there's the fishing.
SUSAN. Never, Henry, have we ever availed ourselves of—I mean profited by the hours when Philip was away fishing.
HENRY. No, certainly not, nor when he was butterflying. I do hope you believe that, old man. (*Leans towards Philip.*)
PHILIP. I really don't see much difference between fishing and the office.
SUSAN. But you go fishing for our daily bread—were it not for that we should starve.
PHILIP. As with the office.
SUSAN. Oh, no, I couldn't bear to think you thought that.
PHILIP. Very well, very well, then I take it that now I am no longer being deceived, so during the fishing hours . . .
SUSAN. Oh, horrid!
HENRY. Really, Philip—this is most embarrassing for us.
PHILIP. (*Rises, crosses downstage.*) I beg your pardon—I apologize for being so tactless. I won't mention it again.
SUSAN. That's a darling. Oh, look, look, see it. (*Points to sky.*) Quick—your hands . . .
HENRY. See what? (*Henry moves to* L. *of Susan, and Philip to her* R., *each gives her his hand.*)
SUSAN. Quick, your hands.
HENRY. Why?
SUSAN. Now, make a wish. Don't talk, close your eyes. Make a wish . . . (*Pause.*) Made it?
HENRY. Yes, made it.
SUSAN. What a phenomenon!
PHILIP. What is it?
SUSAN. Didn't you see it? The white monkey on a tree? An enormous dazzling white monkey. I saw it even with my eyes shut, all the time we were wishing. Then, as soon as we'd wished, it

turned fiery red and disappeared, so we must all have wished the same thing, which will immediately be granted.
PHILIP. Well, I'm not very psychic, and I didn't see the monkey, either dazzling white or fiery red, but I don't mind betting we all wished the same wish.
SUSAN. I know we did. (*Moves to Philip.*) How did you word yours, darling?
PHILIP. I just wished for a ship to come and take us off this island.
SUSAN. Oh. And Henry?
HENRY. (*Turns to Susan.*) I'm afraid I said this bloody island.
SUSAN. Oh.
PHILIP. And you?
HENRY. And you?
SUSAN. (*Sits on log.*) Oh, never mind.
PHILIP. What is it?
HENRY. Come on! Come on!
SUSAN. It really doesn't matter. . . .
PHILIP. You're not crying, are you?
HENRY. What is it, darling?
SUSAN. I—naturally—wished.
PHILIP. Yes?
SUSAN. My—very natural—wish was that you two would be better friends than ever. And in my view it was a much nicer wish than either of yours.
PHILIP. (*Kneels* R. *of Susan.*) Much nicer—it didn't occur to us, that's all.
HENRY. Awfully nice.
SUSAN. But of course, you, being men, can only think about this ship. More important to you, it seems, than our happiness.
PHILIP. Now, darling, that's not fair.
HENRY. The point is we worry about you on this island. I mean, supposing you should get ill, or something.
PHILIP. So we both thought, first, of a ship.
PHILIP *and* HENRY. Because we love you. (*They look at each other, startled, and Susan looks lovingly at them.*)
SUSAN. Oh, you darlings. I shall hug you both. (*She hugs Henry and Philip together. Philip puts arm round her and Henry puts hand on Philip's—both drop arms. Glare at each other.*)
PHILIP. (*Rises.*) Very well then. All right.

SUSAN. All right what?
PHILIP. You can carry on.
SUSAN. Darling, we weren't going to mention that again!
PHILIP. I'm just giving my formal consent.
SUSAN. Good. But don't let's talk about it.
PHILIP. No, well, now you can begin.
SUSAN. Begin what?
PHILIP. Carrying on. (*Picks up pole from tree.*) I'm going fishing.
HENRY. (*Rises.*) Oh, no, Philip, no.
PHILIP. I must, or there won't be any dinner.
HENRY. (*Crosses to Philip.*) But there's no need to stress the fact —no need at all to say going fishing with such a wealth of meaning in your voice.
PHILIP. When I go off after nut-time, with my tackle, it's perfectly obvious where I'm going—it would be very affected to pretend I wasn't.
SUSAN. Announcing it like that, dear, do admit.
HENRY. Yes, it's really most embarrassing for us, Philip.
PHILIP. So it embarrasses you if I fish, now. Really, Henry, you seem determined to be embarrassed.
SUSAN. Just walk away naturally, dear.
PHILIP. I was walking away naturally. I always say when I'm going fishing, you always say when you're going for a swim. Nothing could be more natural.
HENRY. Let's drop the subject, shall we? (*Sits.*)
PHILIP. By all means. You began it. (*Henry sits on log. Philip starts to tiptoe off.*)
SUSAN *and* HENRY. Philip!
PHILIP. (*Turns.*) Now what?
SUSAN. You can't go creeping off like that, it's most indelicate.
PHILIP. May I remind you that I happen to be barefoot. And every step is an agony, and I should also like to point out that I was going off naturally and in silence.
HENRY. (*Rises.*) Well, don't go at all. I think it's very much better if you stay, now.
PHILIP. Really, do you? And what about the dinner?
HENRY. (*Moves to Philip and snatches the rod.*) Damn the dinner!
SUSAN. (*She parts them.*) P'raps you'd better stay, darling. (*Sits on log.*) I think Henry's right.

PHILIP. Would you care to explain your attitude?
HENRY. There's nothing to explain. You've made us feel thoroughly uncomfortable, that's all. (*Philip sits on pumpkin.*)
SUSAN. And as you don't seem able to go fishing in a normally relaxed manner, you'd better stay here for the present.
PHILIP. Certainly! Perhaps you'd like to go and get our dinner today, Henry.
SUSAN. Henry can't fish! Besides, you love your fishing.
PHILIP. Pity we haven't got a pack of cards. A game of Canasta might clear the air.
SUSAN. Why don't you both go down to the beach?
PHILIP. The Walrus and the Carpenter? So like Henry to get us into a muddle and then expect me to get us out.
HENRY. That's right, blame me for everything.
SUSAN. He's not blaming you. He's thinking out loud like when he reorganizes the office.
PHILIP. At the office it's a question of who *works* with whom . . . Here . . .
SUSAN. I know, let me sleep in the little hut, and you two can share the big one.
HENRY. Don't be childish, Susan.
PHILIP. Obviously what is needed here is some form of roster. I remember we had a very good one during the war, when we were fire-watching.
SUSAN. Darling, wouldn't you rather I went for a walk?
PHILIP. Darling, we'll never get anywhere if you keep interrupting. Now, Henry, I think I have the solution to our dilemma. What I suggest is, that for two weeks in each month, Susan should be be a respectable married woman.
HENRY. Steady on, old boy. (*Rises. Crosses to Philip.*)
PHILIP. Wait a minute, Henry. For the other two weeks she remains respectable but she is no longer married.
HENRY. And she has a lover.
PHILIP. That's up to her.
HENRY. Well, that seems eminently fair to me. Tell me, how did you envisage the changeover? Every other week, or every other fortnight?
PHILIP. Oh, you mean should the weeks be alternate or consecutive?
HENRY. Yes, I think so.

PHILIP. Well, I think that is something we should leave to Susan. It will give her an interest. Come, darling. Don't keep us in suspense.
HENRY. I think we've embarrassed her, Philip.
PHILIP. Have we embarrassed you, darling?
HENRY. Had you any sort of preference? Alternate or consecutive?
SUSAN. I feel such a fool. What's the difference?
PHILIP. Alternate would mean every other week . . .
HENRY. And consecutive every other fortnight.
SUSAN. Oh, well, I think alternate would be fairer. After all, we don't know how long we're going to be here, do we?
HENRY. Bravo, Susan, that's quite a point.
SUSAN. (*Rises and crosses to Philip, puts her arms round his neck.*) You are wonderful, Philip. I'm not surprised you get on so well in business. You make it all seem so easy. (*Crosses to Henry, and throws her arms round his neck.*) Henry, Henry, a whole week!
HENRY. (*Puts Susan's arms down.*) Susan, please!
SUSAN. I'm sorry. (*Crosses to Philip.*) Sorry, darling. (*Turns to Henry.*) Still you might look a bit more enthusiastic about Philip's wonderful plan.
HENRY. It's an excellent plan and I'm all for it, but we don't want to be too un-English about it, you know.
PHILIP. Then I take it we're all agreed?
SUSAN. Oh, I am excited for our lovely new life.
PHILIP. I'm sure we all must be. And now would it be quite in order if I were to go fishing?
HENRY. Yes, of course. (*Henry gives rod to Philip.*)
PHILIP. Thank you, Henry. Oh, we may as well start at once. Perhaps you'd better move your things into the big hut.
HENRY. My things?
PHILIP. I was speaking metaphorically.
HENRY. Oh, no, after you, old man.
PHILIP. No, Henry, it's your turn now. (*Exits.*)
SUSAN. (*Moves to Henry, puts her hand to his face.*) Henry, cheer up. It's not very complimentary to me, all this gloom.
HENRY. (*Breaks away.*) Perhaps I have a more sensitive nature than you have. I was thinking of Philip.

SUSAN. But nothing's changed in any way; you said so yourself. Give me a nice kiss and let's be happy about it.
HENRY. (*Looks at Susan.*) Didn't you think he spoke quite sarcastically once or twice?
SUSAN. I'm sure he didn't mean to—it's the blister. He said some terribly nice things about me anyway. (*Looking at Henry's feet.*) And he's given you his shoes, too!
HENRY. Mmm.
SUSAN. (*Puts her left hand to Henry's face.*) And so tonight . . .
HENRY. (*Edging off.*) Yes, well, I think I'll go and help Philip down on the beach. (*Exit.*)
SUSAN. (*Looks after him lovingly as he goes.*) Good idea, my darling. (*Starts gramophone—samba.*) My two darlings!

CURTAIN

ACT II

The same.

A record is heard: "Jungle Birds." Henry sits on the mound juggling with three round fruits. Philip is L. *of mast with his shaving kit. He is not wearing a shirt. He winds his razor, shaves some of the soap froth off his face. Turns off the razor and speaks to Henry.*

PHILIP. Where's the wife? (*With a furious look Henry rises and puts the juggling balls on ground. Susan enters carrying a basket on her head which contains Philip's clean shirt and two clothes pegs. Henry sees her and quickly exits. Philip starts shaving again. Susan crosses to him.*)
SUSAN. Henry, look—look, isn't that good? What have you been doing to poor Henry? He's gone off in the most terrible temper.
PHILIP. Kiss me.
SUSAN. (*Goes to mast, hangs shirt up on clothesline, and pegs the shirt on.*) With that oyster stuff all over your face? I should rather think I won't. Fancy squashing a live oyster on your face. Ugh! How can you!
PHILIP. (*Wiping his face and hands.*) Well, you squash them into your mouth with every appearance of relish. It's my new invention, "oysta-shave," to be produced by the same company as "coco-plast."
SUSAN. (*Puts basket under large leaf.*) Oh, darling, you and your inventions. What did you say to Henry?
PHILIP. I simply asked where you were. (*Faces Susan.*)
SUSAN. (*Rises.*) Naughty, you are. I really must beg of you to stop teasing him, it's so unkind.
PHILIP. You are so pretty when you laugh. (*Moves to Susan.*) Don't go away. Give us a kiss.
SUSAN. Us?
PHILIP. I don't mean us, me and Henry, I mean us, us. (*They kiss.*)

SUSAN. I must get on with the hut work. (*Ties skirt up.*) Today's the day for changing poor Henry's palm leaves and I must see that they are properly aired. We don't want him creaking with rheumatism as well as everything else. (*Goes into hut for turban.*)
PHILIP. (*Goes to mast, picks up talc.*) Do it later.
SUSAN. Why?
PHILIP. I like having you around. There, all the oyster is off, (*Powders face.*) now I pat it with "coco-talc." After shaving try our "coco-talc."
SUSAN. (*Outside hut with turban.*) No, thank you, dear. (*Philip holds out his face to be kissed. Susan goes to mast, puts turban on, looks in mirror on mast.*) You know, whenever I see coconuts at fairs in the future they'll have a very special message for me. I never specially want to be at home again, but there are certain things I rather miss.
PHILIP. Poor darling, what?
SUSAN. Fogs, for instance.
PHILIP. I can't say I miss fogs.
SUSAN. Policemen is another, and now, I am reminded by all these coconuts. (*Picks up nuts.*) Carnival! (*Throws coconuts off stage.*) Don't you remember, throwing the coconuts and the dodgems and . . .
PHILIP. Dodgems? (*Puts left arm round Susan's waist, bounces with her.*) I'll dodgem you—why didn't you say so before. (*Bumps round with her, picks her up and swings her round.*)
SUSAN. Stop—Philip—you're killing me, stop—stop!
PHILIP. Oh, I know half the fun is saying stop and it doesn't stop.
SUSAN. Darling—darling——! (*Both fall on floor, Susan half across Philip. Enter Henry, panting. Henry has tropical creeper coiled round him.*)
HENRY. What on earth's the matter? I could hear your screams all the way from the top of the date palms. I've never been so frightened. Thought something awful was happening. It's too bad of you, Philip; I wish you wouldn't do that.
SUSAN. It was awful—that awful Philip pretending to be a dodgems. I'm all black and blue.
PHILIP. Henry, I must know what you are going as!
SUSAN. (*Sitting up.*) Well, go back to your dates, my darling, we won't disturb you again, I promise.
HENRY. I'm not sure I shall ever be able to climb a palm again.

SUSAN. Why on earth not?
HENRY. I fell the last fifty feet. I think I've broken my back. I heard it crack.
SUSAN. Nonsense, my darling, if you've broken your back you'd look all crooked.
PHILIP. (*Rises and moves to Henry.*) He does look a bit crooked to me. The best thing you can do is to have a nice paddle and cool yourself off.
HENRY. No. I'm going straight back up that palm before I lose my nerve. (*Exits.*)
SUSAN. He's in a sulk. Well, I'm off.
PHILIP. (*To Susan.*) Don't go.
SUSAN. Now what?
PHILIP. I like looking at you.
SUSAN. (*Crosses to mast and puts leaves down under large leaf.*) Isn't your shirt dry yet?
PHILIP. Why?
SUSAN. You're much prettier with your shirt on, you know. Like this anyone would think you were an unemployed baker.
PHILIP. I'll put my coat on.
SUSAN. But you'll die of heat. You were all right really. (*Tidies shirt on line.*)
PHILIP. (*Takes tray from mast and puts it in hut.*) I don't care to look like an unemployed baker.
SUSAN. (*Pulls gramophone cord. Waltz music starts.*) What pinnacle of manly beauty do you aim at?
PHILIP. (*Comes out of hut to* C. *of stage.*) I wish to look like your husband.
SUSAN. (*Crosses to Philip.*) Aren't you a darling! (*He puts his arms round her and they waltz.*) Only no more dodgems, I beg.
PHILIP. You know you loved it.
SUSAN. I might love it later in the day when I'm not quite so busy.
PHILIP. I've quite finished shaving, so may I kiss you?
SUSAN. You want to kiss me because you've finished shaving?
PHILIP. It's as good a reason as any other.
SUSAN. You say that all the time.
PHILIP. I want to kiss you all the time. All day long, ever since my week began.

SUSAN. So I've noticed. (*They kiss. Susan moves to* L. *mound and gets leaves.*)
PHILIP. We are happy, aren't we?
SUSAN. Madly.
PHILIP. How d'you account for it?
SUSAN. Well, we are a happily married couple. (*She puts palm leaves on floor, sits on one and starts to sew patch on the other.*) I suppose it's the happiest thing there is.
PHILIP. (*Sits* R. *of Susan.*) Poor you, all that hut work. I sometimes wonder if it's not too much for you. Next time it's my week on, how about a little holiday?
SUSAN. Holiday?
PHILIP. I've found such a pretty bay where we can swim and lie in the sun all day. We'll have to camp out of course.
SUSAN. I'd love it.
PHILIP. Would you really?
SUSAN. Love it. But of course we can't.
PHILIP. Why not?
SUSAN. Because of Henry. (*Sews leaf.*) It's very naughty and disloyal to leave poor Henry alone, when you can see how sad he's feeling.
PHILIP. I don't know why. Everything on this island is arranged to suit him. Let's make him an apple-pie bed!
SUSAN. It's his week off he's hating so much.
PHILIP. He was exactly the same during his week on.
SUSAN. I think he felt guilty all the time then. Henry broods over things, you know. He has complexes. Anyway I understand him.
PHILIP. I don't, but I love him when he's in a rage, he's so funny. So are you, when you're in a rage.
SUSAN. Except I never am.
PHILIP. (*Rises.*) Oh, no, never.
SUSAN. It's my great charm, nothing ever makes me angry.
PHILIP. Nothing? I say . . . !
SUSAN. What?
PHILIP. Give me your hands . . .
SUSAN. (*Rises and gives him both hands.*) Why?
PHILIP. Shut your eyes.
SUSAN. Open my mouth?
PHILIP. No. Make a wish.
SUSAN. Right.

PHILIP. Made it?
SUSAN. Mm.
PHILIP. (*Ecstatically.*) What a phenomenon.
SUSAN. (*Suspiciously.*) What is all this?
PHILIP. You didn't see it?
SUSAN. See what?
PHILIP. An enormous dazzling white monkey on a stick in the sky.
SUSAN. Oh, you brute. (*She bits him, and he runs upstage round the bluebell tree, and under the leaf at the* R. *Susan follows him, speaking as they go.*) Phenomenon indeed—I might have known—you couldn't see a phenomenon from your own nose.
PHILIP. Help—help—Henry—Henry —— Ow, that really hurt! You're biting my ear —— Henry! Henry! (*Henry enters.*) It's all right, Henry, we're in the summer house! (*Henry looks furious and exits the way he entered. Susan comes from under leaf and runs into hut, then looks out of window.*) Didn't you see it turn fiery red and disappear? I mean the monkey, not Henry. Now, don't sulk, darling, it doesn't suit you.
SUSAN. I hate you to make fun of the occult.
PHILIP. (*Kneeling outside window.*) I never will again. I promise.
SUSAN. (*At window.*) It's most dangerous to trifle with the unseen.
PHILIP. I'm truly penitent.
SUSAN. I wish you could see yourself, an old married man like you, skipping round in evening trousers playing childish tricks on people. (*Disappears from window into back of hut.*)
PHILIP. (*Rises and moves in front of hut door.*) Come here, darling.
SUSAN. No.
PHILIP. I want to apologize.
SUSAN. You needn't bother.
PHILIP. Do kiss and be friends.
SUSAN. (*Enters from hut and goes to look in mirror on mast.*) I shall never kiss you again.
PHILIP. Then we must be divorced.
SUSAN. Sooner the better.
PHILIP. (*Crosses to Susan.*) Darling—I never saw the shadow of a white monkey. I promise.
SUSAN. Telephone! (*Philip turns round quickly as if to go and*

answer it, and then remembers, stops and turns to Susan. She shrieks.)
PHILIP. (*Really angry for a minute.*) You are maddening, Susan, when you do that.
SUSAN. It always works—it always works. (*Clapping her hands.*)
PHILIP. Exceedingly funny.
SUSAN. Now, you're in a sulk.
PHILIP. I'm not in a sulk at all, I'm very angry indeed.
SUSAN. Temper, temper.
PHILIP. And you must be punished.
SUSAN. Catch me first. Help! Help! Murder! Help, Henry! (*Susan runs upstage to behind hut, with Philip following her.*)
PHILIP. (*As he chases her.*) Henry! Henry! Stop her! (*He doubles back and she runs on. She tries to get on at entrance below but but he is there, then she tries the entrance downstage and as she runs on he catches her, puts her across his knee and slaps her. As he smacks her.*) One, two, three, four, five, six . . . (*Henry enters, turns and moves across the stage during the smacking.*)
SUSAN. Oh, you really are hurting.
PHILIP. Yes, I mean to. Seven, eight, nine, ten, eleven, twelve.
HENRY. Midnight. (*Exits.*)
SUSAN. (*Rises and kneels on floor.*) Darling Philip, I'll never do it again.
PHILIP. Say you're sorry.
SUSAN. (*Kneeling.*) Sorry.
PHILIP. Promise to revere your husband.
SUSAN. Promise to revere my husband.
PHILIP. Promise never to do the telephone trick again, and try and be a better girl in future.
SUSAN. Is that all?
PHILIP. All?
SUSAN. I was awfully afraid you were going to kiss me.
PHILIP. That was not part of the punishment.
SUSAN. Oh, good. (*Rises and faces him.*)
PHILIP. (*Catching her round the waist.*) What did you say? Look at me. Now—do you love me?
SUSAN. I love you like mad. (*They kiss passionately. Henry enters from behind hut carrying fruit and leaves over a stick of bamboo. He watches them kiss.*)
HENRY. (*Scowling.*) *Pardonnez moi!*

PHILIP. (*Looks at him.*) Oh, there's Uncle Henry. (*Moves to* R. *and sits juggling with the balls.*)
SUSAN. (*Takes fruit off of stick.*) Oh, you've got my order, nuts, dates, avocadoes, vine, leaves, aubergenes. Are they fresh in today? What? No truffles?
HENRY. *C'est pas possible.*
SUSAN. Oh, I was going to do coconut *à la temps perdue.*
HENRY. You'll just have to do coconut *à l'autre chose.*
SUSAN. Haven't you got one teeny weeny truffle under the counter? (*Susan goes to mast with nuts.*)
HENRY. I don't think there's a truffle, teeny or weeny left on the island.
PHILIP. Henry, look! Self taught! (*Juggling with two balls.*)
HENRY. Philip, look! (*Balances the stick on his foot, and places his hat on top of the stick.*)
SUSAN. Oh, if only we had one of those darling little pigs on a lead with a ring through its nose.
PHILIP. We can't have everything—we're got Henry. What would be the good of that?
SUSAN. Darling, that's how they find truffles in France.
PHILIP. If we had a darling little pig on a lead with a ring through its nose I should vote for roast pork. (*Henry hangs his hat on the hut.*)
SUSAN. As we're not having roast pork, darling, you'd better go and prepare the coconuts, and light me a fire.
PHILIP. Yes, my darling.
SUSAN. But be careful with the lighter, it's nearly empty.
PHILIP. (*Rises and moves to the* C.) What do we do when we run out of petrol?
SUSAN. (*Kneels and puts juggling balls into box.*) Rub two sticks together of course.
HENRY. (*Balancing stick on foot.*) You don't believe that non-sense, do you?
PHILIP. Certainly we do, on that simple faith the entire Boy Scout movement was founded. (*Drops stick which he has picked up on "Boy Scout" on Henry's foot and exits below hut.*) Be prepared. (*Giving Boy Scout salute.*)
HENRY. Delightful.
SUSAN. (*Sits on pumpkin, picks up shell bag from mound.*) What is?

HENRY. Every time I arrive I find you two tousling each other, makes me feel horribly in the way.
SUSAN. Oh—oh—you're not cross?
HENRY. (*Balancing stick.*) Cross! I'm hurt and angry—and I think I've got every reason to be.
SUSAN. Why take any notice?
HENRY. My dear Susan, how can I help it?
SUSAN. Then don't keep boo-ing out at us. (*Powders.*)
HENRY. I don't boo out at you, this part of the island is our sitting room and I must be able to walk into it without the risk of being treated to an embarrassing scene.
SUSAN. Oh, dear. . . .
HENRY. I should never have expected Philip to behave like this. He makes me feel *de trop* every time I come near you.
SUSAN. I suppose we can play at dodgems if we want to. (*Puts on lipstick.*)
HENRY. You weren't playing dodgems then.
SUSAN. I suppose I may kiss my husband if I want to?
HENRY. It isn't kissing your husband, you are both behaving as if you were passionately in love all of a sudden. He makes love to you all day—every word, every look—you might be on your honeymoon. It's unbearable. (*Turns to mast.*)
SUSAN. But darling Henry, it's his week on, do admit.
HENRY. Week on, indeed. And during my week on, as you call it, did I ever behave like that? You know quite well I did not.
SUSAN. P'raps he's more in love with me than you were.
HENRY. He's no right to be in love—he's your husband. (*Balances stick on his chin.*)
SUSAN. (*Puts bag down on her* L., *tucks dress up.*) It's absolutely nothing to do with you if my lawful wedded husband happens to be in love with me after eight years of marriage. Flattering, really. (*Rises and crosses to Henry, hangs fruit on hut.*) I must get on with the hut work.
HENRY. (*Picks up yellow pumpkin, and places it as pillow on mound.*) Too bad of Philip. I took an infinity of trouble not to upset him during my week, and this is my reward. (*Sits.*) He behaves exactly as if you and he were alone together on this utterly bloody island.
SUSAN. But, darling, he is my husband, do admit.
HENRY. Nobody'd ever think of it. I'm the deadly old husband in

this outfit—you two behave as if you were in the throes of first love. Why, Philip has taken on a new lease of life—he looks ten years younger.
SUSAN. (*Still putting fruit on hut.*) Doesn't he look wonderful! Even in that extraordinary getup. It's wonderful because he's so happy. He laughs and jokes because he's happy all day, and I laugh and joke with him, because I'm happy too. (*Picks up one palm leaf, leaves the other on the floor.*) Oh, the heaven of being happy.
HENRY. Do stop saying "happy" in that voice—if you knew how affected it sounds.
SUSAN. Disagreeable-you-are. (*Goes to hut with leaf.*)
HENRY. There is something really sinister about all this happiness.
SUSAN. (*Re-enters, puts on apron.*) Don't you want us to be happy?
HENRY. Yes, within reason. (*Susan exits to hut, puts leaf in and gets pan and brush.*) But I don't like this atmosphere of amorous conspiracy. I feel left out of everything. Not very nice for me.
SUSAN. (*Brushing the outside of the hut.*) It may not have been very nice for Philip either, sleeping all alone in the little hut, but was he ever cross or embarrassed? Not for a moment—you had to admit yourself that he was perfect. (*Goes to mast.*) Yet he must have suffered, you know.
HENRY. Suffered? He didn't mind a scrap.
SUSAN. Oh?
HENRY. I know Philip. He can't keep anything under his hat; out it all comes with him. I don't believe he gave you a single thought last week, not one.
SUSAN. All right. (*Sweeps ladder.*) Then what's upsetting you?
HENRY. His behavior now, of course. He's having his revenge by showing me that he's the one who really counts in your life. (*Susan crosses to Henry, brushes mound, then brushes leaves.*) It's very subtle and terribly cruel and it's killing me by inches.
SUSAN. My darling Henry, you've just said yourself that Philip is incapable of dissimulation—everything comes out, with him. (*Henry picks up leaf, and Susan stops.*) Henry, nobody's going to look under there. (*Pulls Henry up, sweeps under him.*) I'm beginning to think you are going just a tiny bit mad.
HENRY. Perhaps I am. (*Puts melon downstage.*)
SUSAN. You're not jealous, by any chance?

HENRY. But my dear girl, that's what I'm trying to tell you. Of course I am, terribly, insanely jealous. I love you, Susan, I adore you, I'm in a most miserable state.
SUSAN. Oh, dear. Poor you.
HENRY. I'm in agony. Every time he goes near you I want to sock him on the jaw. (*He makes pass at leaf with stick.*)
SUSAN. Well, I beg you won't.
HENRY. I try and control myself, for your sake, but I really can't say what will happen if this goes on.
SUSAN. Gracious! Now what? After all, the whole thing was your idea, do you admit?
HENRY. Yes, and a terribly bad one. Anyhow, it can't go on like this, and I shall speak to Philip.
SUSAN. Not again!
HENRY. (*Moves to Susan.*) Yes, I must, and he must think of a new arrangement. You don't want me to have a nervous breakdown, I suppose?
SUSAN. I think Philip will be fed up with all this speaking, (*Up on mound, throws dust.*) and I'm quite sure he won't bother about a new arrangement. He likes this one as it is.
HENRY. Very well then, I shall have to go.
SUSAN. Go? Where?
HENRY. Just take my chance in the jungle, as many a brave man has before me.
SUSAN. Goodness! Don't pocket the razor, will you, we need it here.
HENRY. What a heart of stone you have, Susan! Anyhow, Philip is the master of my fate. I shall explain the whole thing to him. Either he accepts my proposition or I shall just stumble away into the unknown for ever.
SUSAN. Oh, you've *got* a proposition, then?
HENRY. Yes. Your idea.
SUSAN. Mine?
HENRY. (*Onto mound facing Susan.*) You suggested it, if you remember, that Philip and I might share the big hut and you live in the little one.
SUSAN. All alone?
HENRY. Far the best. In future we must live like brothers and sisters—it's the only way.
SUSAN. We must, must we?

HENRY. Well, until the ship comes, anyhow.
SUSAN. Well, my darling Henry, I'm very sorry you're going mad and all that, but the time has come for a little plain speaking. Philip and I have pandered to you quite long enough, and I can tell you straight away that he will never treat me as a sister—never. Sister indeed! Have you ever seen Philip's sister? *(Off mound and into hut.)*
HENRY. But it would be the same for both of us.
SUSAN. *(Coming out of hut, pulls dress down again.)* That's too generous of you. I guess Philip's answer will be that you can treat me as a sister until you're blue in the face, but that he intends to treat me as a wife, which is what I happen to be. And there's just one other point—I am also a citizen, a voter, a tax-payer, a grown-up woman and a British subject by marriage. I happen to be very good-natured, and you can boss me about to a certain extent but not without limit and the limit has now been reached. So will you please note that the present arrangement suits me *very well.* *(Goes to hut.)*
HENRY. Hm.
SUSAN. Very well indeed. It could have been made for me.
HENRY. *(Sits by mast.)* And you can enjoy seeing me goaded to my grave.
SUSAN. Grave now! You know, Henry, when we get home I shall have to take you to a psychiatrist.
HENRY. In fact my wretchedness rather amuses you.
SUSAN. Henry—if you go on like this I really might say something.
HENRY. You're delighted by this change in Philip.
SUSAN. *(Moves to Henry.)* It's not a change. Philip has always loved me. *(Kneels on mound.)*
HENRY. And that I'm left out in the cold.
SUSAN. But of course, on your week off. You knew it would be like that. *(Leans on Henry's shoulder.)* Only four more days, dearest, then it'll be your week on again.
HENRY. Dearest! That's what you call Philip when he's lost the keys on the car. *(Philip can be heard singing off stage "Old Man River" and "If You Were the Only Girl.")* I've become the dull old husband now with a vengeance.
SUSAN. Now I'm going off to cook the dinner, and I'd like you to

have a serious think about what I've said, because I've meant it all, every word. (*Rises.*)
HENRY. Why don't you say outright that I get on your nerves?
SUSAN. Well, you do when you make horrid scenes. I hate all these complications—you're not reasonable. Never mind. (*Enter Philip from behind hut with two nuts on sticks with faces painted on them.*)
PHILIP. Come on, darling. Your little victims are ready for you. They died bravely.
SUSAN. Oh, clever you. When we get home you must have an exhibition.
PHILIP. I don't think I'm quite ready for that yet, dear.
SUSAN. Now, I suppose I've got to go and roast myself over that beastly fire. (*Takes nuts.*)
PHILIP. Not yourself, dear, just the nuts.
SUSAN. I'll probably burn everything—I'm in a thoroughly bad temper, let me tell you. (*Exits behind hut.*)
PHILIP. Have you been teasing her too? I wish you'd been there just now when I pretended to see a white monkey—she went for me tooth and nail. Adorable, isn't she? I can't remember the time when we've been so happy, and I really think it's all due to you, Henry. (*Goes upstage to behind clothesline.*) I never would have thought of this experiment myself—well, naturally not—but it's had most interesting results. (*Feels shirt.*) Oh, good, my shirt is dry. Yes, as I was saying, how right you were to insist—how sensible really, we've both been over all this. Think what a fuss some men would have made in my place, and how wrong they would have been. D'you mind if I dress for dinner? (*Gets shirt from clothesline. As he unpegs it the rope breaks.*) Oh, bother, I've broken the clothesline. One simply doesn't know one's own strength! (*Puts scarf on ladder.*) Yes, I'd like every husband in the world to have our receipt. (*Puts shirt on.*) Shaken out of his complacency by the knowledge that his wife is loved by another man, the husband suddenly realizes two things; first, that he may be in danger of losing her for ever; secondly, that he must now be a lover again as well as a husband. Clearly we ought to get away from the formula of one wife, one husband—much to be said for polygamy. I'm sure that's the coming thing now, like television. Look at me—I feel twenty years younger, and Susan has never been so happy. And why? Simply because of you. For a marriage

to be really happy one must be three—I can see it now clearly as daylight. The fact that you and Susan are, well, the same as me and Susan, makes me ten times more in love and not a bit jealous. Isn't that strange? Shirt's not too bad, considering it hasn't been ironed, is it? I shall have to give the makers a testimonial when we get home or perhaps I could write it now and bottle it. Henry! Henry! (*Henry becomes aware of him.*) We were cut off. Penny for your thoughts, Henry, old man.
HENRY. I'm thinking over what you've just said.
PHILIP. I thought it sounded very well. I think I shall take up a post as Professor of Sex Education when we get home.
HENRY. (*Rises.*) Well, old boy. *No.*
PHILIP. No, I wasn't serious, of course.
HENRY. No. This isn't the right way.
PHILIP. No, you must keep your head down!
HENRY. No, I mean the way we've been living. You and me and Susan.
PHILIP. But it was arranged entirely to suit you!
HENRY. I know. I can't stand it.
PHILIP. You keep not being able to stand things. It makes life very difficult. Didn't you enjoy your week?
HENRY. No.
PHILIP. You had such lovely weather for it, too. Why not?
HENRY. I could only think about you.
PHILIP. Me?
HENRY. I reproached myself terribly for having told you. Never should I have done such a thing.
PHILIP. I don't agree at all. (*Goes to leaf on floor and sits.*) And now you know that I am deeply satisfied with the present state of affairs, does that not make a difference?
HENRY. (*Facing Philip.*) Unfortunately, Philip, I have a sensitive nature, and was perfectly well able to imagine what you must have been suffering.
PHILIP. Suffering? When?
HENRY. Last week of course.
PHILIP. Oh! Oh, no—not a bit, not a bit.
HENRY. Alone in your hut? Lying awake and . . .
PHILIP. No, no, you should have asked me, you shouldn't have worried like this. Never slept so well in my life. There's something about this place. I cannot keep awake. The air, perhaps.

HENRY. (*Leans forward over Philip.*) But Susan—weren't you thinking about her at all?
PHILIP. Not particularly! I just snored, you know.
HENRY. You snored?
PHILIP. Yes.
HENRY. Thinking of nothing? Not missing Susan?
PHILIP. I pretended that Susan was staying with her mother.
HENRY. Not jealous of me?
PHILIP. My dear old boy, never gave you a thought.
HENRY. Rubbish! (*Goes up to hut, puts stick against it.*)
PHILIP. Why?
HENRY. I know what it is to be in love.
PHILIP. Yes, but as you took hours and hours explaining to me the other day, nothing has changed. You've been part of our life for six years, why should I be tortured by jealousy now? Not logical.
HENRY. (*Kneels next to Philip.*) Logical! All right then, you don't mind me, but supposing another man should arrive on this island and begin making love to Susan? Do you mean to say you still wouldn't mind? (*Rises.*)
PHILIP. I don't know what I'd feel. The same set of circumstances doesn't apply to that situation, and I've no idea how I should feel about it. All I know is that once I have accepted something as perfectly logical I can't begin being put out by it just to please you.
HENRY. (*Leans over Philip.*) And if Susan had four lovers, or eight, all taking turns in the hut, would you still feel twenty years younger?
PHILIP. Susan is not the daughter of the regiment.
HENRY. I'm carrying your thesis to its extreme, to show you how purely asinine it is.
PHILIP. Your thesis, not mine.
HENRY. Oh, you'll drive me mad! Perhaps it was mine, perhaps in a moment of idiocy I may have put forward some argument, well, now I see that I made a terrible mistake.
PHILIP. No, nonsense.
HENRY. I should never have told you, never. And if I hadn't been blinded by love I would have seen where telling you would lead us, because of course it's not true to say that nothing is changed.

The moment you knew everything was changed, you knew instead of not knowing, and that made the whole difference.

PHILIP. I can't follow this. Granted everything is changed for me—but for you nothing's changed. I never kept it a secret that Susan was my wife—I was perfectly frank about it. When I introduced you I said, "Henry, this is my wife." It may not have been a very original introduction but it was perfectly clear. So what the hell are you complaining about? (*Rises and moves toward Henry.*)

HENRY. (*Backing away.*) Steady on, old chap, I've got a very reasonable proposition to put to you, but we must keep calm.

PHILIP. I know—you'd like me to give up Susan altogether.

HENRY. Yes, just for the time being, old boy.

PHILIP. For the time being?

HENRY. Till the ship comes along.

PHILIP. You'd like me to go and live in the little hut until the ship comes along.

HENRY. No, no, you haven't understood. My idea is that we should all live like brothers and sisters for the rest of the time we have to be on this island.

PHILIP. But you *were* living like her brother, that was what the fuss was about. You said you couldn't stand it—I wish I knew what it is you could stand.

HENRY. Please listen to me, Philip. I'm in dead earnest. *Susan must live in the little hut.*

PHILIP. And you and me together in the big hut? Oh, no, my dear old boy. I'm very fond of you and all that, but no. I can't agree to that. (*Stops suddenly.*) By the way, this proposition, have you put it to Susan?

HENRY. Yes, I have.

PHILIP. And I suppose she's on your side as usual?

HENRY. Well, not exactly. That is, in this case, Susan, darling Susan, doesn't see quite eye to eye with me.

PHILIP. Indeed?

HENRY. No. And—what about you, Philip?

PHILIP. Me? I am categorically against it; you needn't mention that one again. I've behaved very well to you—more than well—nobly—since we arrived here; I've lent you Susan, and given you my shoes. (*To ladder* R. *of mast, gets tie.*)

HENRY. You call it noble to refuse the hand of friendship when I'm so unhappy? (*Goes to hut.*)

PHILIP. (*Putting on tie.*) But, Henry, because I love Susan and Susan loves me that doesn't mean you've lost her, you know. Why, only last night we discussed you for hours, and I wish you could have heard what we said—you'd have been proud. I remember thinking at the time—if only old Henry could hear all this it would quite set him up.

HENRY. So you talk about me when you are together. "Dear old Henry," I suppose! It's the absolute and utter last straw! No woman who's in love ever discusses her lover with her husband, it's quite the other way round. Can you wonder I'm nervous and upset with this sort of thing going on? (*Stamping his feet.*)

PHILIP. Very well, we won't discuss you again. I promise. (*Gets leaf and folds it.*)

HENRY. So you refuse my proposition.

PHILIP. Yes, I do. But cheer up, Henry, only four more days and I shall be back in the little hut again.

HENRY. I don't care two hoots in hell for the little hut and who is in it. That's not the point.

PHILIP. And what is the point?

HENRY. The point is, that when I'm in the little hut I suffer, and when you're in the little hut you only snore.

PHILIP. Henry, it's better to be snoring than boring!

HENRY. Smug and facetious as usual. You're a great thick-skinned bully, and that's my last word.

PHILIP. That was very rude.

HENRY. I only hope that some chap will come along one day and really put the horns on you and then perhaps you'll begin to understand—and suffer! (*Knocks leaf out of Philip's hand and exits* R.)

PHILIP. Friendly. (*Picks up straw shoes.*) It's better to be snoring than boring. I must tell Susan that. (*To ladder to pick up straw cravat, then towards the little hut. Goes towards big hut, still carrying the leaf, his shoes, and the cravat. Exit into hut. An arrow whistles onto the mast from* D. L. *followed by a handsome, sunburnt young man clad in a loin cloth and a feathered head dress. He has a lei of flowers hanging from his right hip. He carries a bow. He stands* D. L. *like a statue with the bow in his left hand Philip comes out of the hut putting his coat on and singing "Just Susan and me and Henry makes three." He looks round for a flower to put in his buttonhole, sees the lei, and pulls a flower off the foot of it, fixes it in his buttonhole, moving towards the mirror on the mast. He looks into the mirror, then more closely, takes out his handkerchief, and wipes his face. Turns upstage, humming, so that the feathers on the end of the arrow tickle his neck. He slaps his neck a couple of times, but cannot get rid of it, so he turns and sees the arrow. He runs his fingers along the arrow, puzzled, and then following the direction it arrived from, he sees The Stranger standing on the top of the mound, screams and runs upstage. He returns down the* R. *side of the mast to the mound.*) Good afternoon, my dear fellow, how do you do? (*Louder.*) How do you do? Good afternoon. (*The Stranger bows, one hand on shoulder, Philip bows to him.*) A little language difficulty. (*The Stranger bows again, and Philip bows as he does.*) It's no use going on with "good afternoon," it's probably evening by now. (*A step forward—The Stranger bows slightly forward.*) Would you excuse me if I bring up reinforcements? Don't run away now, there's a good fellow. (*Goes off* U. L. *shouting.*) Henry! Henry! (*Henry enters* R.)

HENRY. I'm coming. You know I want to apologize for . . . My dear fellow, for goodness' sake, put your trousers on. (*Sees Stranger, bolts off* R. *shouting.*) Philip! Philip! (*Enter Susan from* U. L. *behind hut. She is carrying two large palm leaves which prevent her from seeing The Stranger until she is* C. *stage. Stranger leans the bow against the tree behind him.*)

SUSAN. Do say I'm wonderful . . . done the cooking and found all these lovely new sheets. (*Sees The Stranger, screams. Stranger bows, stops dead and drops the leaves. She examines him, and lets out an "oh" of undisguised admiration and curtsies. The Stranger on the mound bows with a hand on each shoulder respectfully. Susan curtsies again.*) Who are you? The King? King of the Island? Or the Crown Prince, perhaps? (*As he bows.*) The Crown Prince! Oh, sir, we are honored. (*He advances towards her. She rises and backs to the mast. She is embarrassed.*) Oh . . . nothing . . . (*Backing to mast.*) I didn't mean . . . I just wondered. Please don't think it hateful of me. (*Sees the arrow.*) But you're not cannibals in your family, by any chance? (*He takes the lei and holds it out to her.*) So kind—I don't know if I ought to (*He indicates that she must kneel down, which she does.*) but . . . If your Royal Highness insists . . . (*He puts the flowers on her*

head and gives her his hands to help her up again.) Thank you, sir, thank you very much. They're lovely.
PHILIP. (*Off stage.*) Henry!
HENRY. (*Off stage.*) Philip! (*The Stranger leaps back onto the mound and picks up his bow, and stands as on his first entrance.*)
SUSAN. Oh, sir, I must explain. They're just doing their exercises. I am staying here with my husband and my lover, our friend, I mean. (*Philip and Henry start shouting for each other off stage.*) They're making rather a noise, I'm afraid. (*Philip runs across the stage behind huts from* R. *to* L., *shouting.*) No need to shout, we can hear you. (*Philip enters from the* L. *Henry enters from the* R. *and meets Philip. They clasp each other.*)
PHILIP *and* HENRY. (*Together.*) Oh, there you are. You've seen him?
SUSAN. Sir, may I present my husband, my lo . . . our friend, the Crown Prince. (*They look at her.*)
PHILIP. Why—has he spoken?
SUSAN. No. It's not necessary.
HENRY. What's he been up to?
SUSAN. Nothing. He bows and he's given me these lovely flowers to show that he is on our side. (*Henry takes Susan's hand.*) The custom, I expect, at his father's court. (*Henry bows to Stranger.*)
PHILIP. What are you doing?
HENRY. Making myself known, old boy.
PHILIP. There, you see, the island is very big, and there are natives in the hinterland, exactly as I supposed.
HENRY. It may be as big as America, for all we know.
PHILIP. I suppose it couldn't be America?
HENRY. I wonder.
PHILIP. (*Looks at The Stranger.*) No. We must find some way of conversing with Hiawatha. (*He advances slowly and starts to recite "By the shores of Gitchiguma." The Stranger slaps at a fly on the back of his neck, then rubs his nose. Philip and Henry run to* R. *of mast. Pulling himself together.*) I frightened him. (*A step forward.*) Are you dumb?
SUSAN. Speak!
HENRY. Speak!
PHILIP. No speak!
SUSAN. Maybe he doesn't understand English!
HENRY. Oh, he must.

SUSAN. *Parlez vous français?*
HENRY. *Sprechen Sie deutsch?*
PHILIP. (*To Henry.*) Not much good if he does *sprechen*, none of us do. He's clearly no linguist.
HENRY. You don't think he's half-witted, do you?
PHILIP. The island idiot.
SUSAN. (*Scornfully.*) Really, what rubbish. Just look at him.
HENRY. (*Loudly.*) Well, he doesn't exactly radiate intelligence, you know. Why does he stand there rooted to the spot? (*The Stranger looks at them and bows.*)
PHILIP. He's the original "Yes" man, isn't he?
SUSAN. He's got a sweet nature, you can see that.
HENRY. Sounds are no good, we must try signs. (*Moves to mast, holding on with left hand.*) How about something to eat? (*Points to his mouth.*)
PHILIP. Henry! Don't give him ideas. (*The Stranger shakes his head.*)
HENRY. You see, he understood that at once. This is the way.
SUSAN. Clever Henry!
PHILIP. Well, now ask him, by signs, how many inhabitants there are on the island, where they live, whether their houses have got bathrooms, and what they can do . . . (*The Stranger jumps off the mound and goes to the mast. Philip moves upstage, Henry grabs Susan and moves downstage with her. Stranger leaves his bow on the mound. He takes the arrow out of the mast and puts it in the sheath. Then he looks at the mast.*)
SUSAN. He's looking at our mast.
PHILIP. Big stick, what? (*The Stranger picks up the clothesline.*)
HENRY. That's our string, (*Picks up string and stretches is across Philip.*) string for the washing, stringy, stringy, wash, wash. (*Philip hangs his handkerchief on the line. Stranger takes a step towards it.*)
PHILIP. You've hit on something there—say it again, Henry.
HENRY. Stringy, stringy, wash-wash! (*The Stranger runs his hand along the line, as he almost reaches the handkerchief Philip snatches it. "Waar!" The Stranger barks at them, and Henry and Philip run into the hut. Susan goes upstage of mound to hut. The Stranger stands* R. *of mast, puts one hand up against the mast, and steps away, keeping his hand where it was as if to measure his height. He barks, and beckons Philip towards the mast, swinging*

his hand towards the mast. Barks "Um de ga woom, Bah-a woom bah!")

PHILIP. Henry, you're wanted. (*Stranger barks again.*) Does he want to measure me? (*Stranger barks again.*)

SUSAN. I know—his father the King has a regiment of head-hunters and he wants to see if you're tall enough for it.

PHILIP. Not at all sure I want to join up again, you know, had about enough last time. (*"Ah woom. Bah Wha," The Stranger barks; claps his hands and points to the mast. Philip creeps back toward hut. Susan crosses to hut doorway.*)

SUSAN. Oh, don't start annoying him, whatever happens. (*To Stranger.*) My husband is honored, sir, for your Royal Highness to measure him. Go on, darling. (*Pulls Philip. The Stranger barks and beckons again. Philip goes across to the mast and stands with his back to it facing front.*)

PHILIP. (*As he goes.*) All right. (*The Stranger barks again, and indicates to Henry that he is to come, too.*)

HENRY. (*Looking out over top of hut doorway.*) Tell him I've been drafted! (*Stranger barks again. Henry comes out of hut.*) Well, I suppose if he gave us commissions straight away and we both had orderlies . . . (*"Ah woom bah." The Stranger advances towards him, clapping his hands. Henry moves downstage to mast.*) All right, don't get excited—six foot one in my socks. (*The Stranger looks at them, then moves swiftly across to the* L. *Stands there, puts up hands.*) I think he's going to take our photograph. (*Then starts his dance moving up and round the mast counter-clockwise. As he goes downstage. The Stranger has gone round the mast twice; each time he goes round, Henry goes before him trying to get out of his way close to mast.*)

PHILIP. Wait, Henry, he'll come round. (*The Stranger goes around once more.*) I think it's a kind of samba. (*He joins in the dance, following The Stranger round and copying him.*) Come on, Henry, don't be a wallflower! (*Henry joins in the dance. The Stranger gets ahead of the other two, and as they reach stage* L. *of the mast, he picks up the end of the net, they dance into it and he ties them up. During the tying up Philip and Henry scream for Susan, who is laughing at them.*) What are you doing? White man not pleased. Help, Susan; Susan, do something!

SUSAN. (*Goes across to mast.*) What can I do? Serves you right for mocking him.

HENRY. That's it, take his side. Absolutely typical—here we are tied up like a bunch of asparagus. For all you know he's going to burn us at the stake.
SUSAN. Does he look like a *cannibal?* (*Trying to untie them. The Stranger, who has been facing front turns towards her.*) You ought never to have upset him.
PHILIP. Did we upset him?
SUSAN. Making all those signs and noises. I wish you could have seen yourselves mouthing like a pair of lunatics while he stood, clothed only in his savage dignity. Can't you see that he is exceptional?
HENRY. Of course. A Crown Prince.
SUSAN. Yes. You offended him deeply and he wanted to show that he was stronger than both of you put together. (*To Stranger.*) Didn't Your Royal Highness? (*The Stranger turns* R., *faces Susan and holds out his right hand.*) Oh, Philip. He's holding out his hand.
PHILIP. Then shake it, dear. We don't want to be here for ever. (*Susan crosses to Stranger and takes his hand, whereupon he moves to her* R. *quickly and urges her toward the hut. She edges away from him.*)
SUSAN. What does he want?
HENRY. (*Who cannot see her.*) What's happening? Do keep up a running commentary.
SUSAN. Oh, Philip . . .
PHILIP. Has he said anything?
SUSAN. It isn't that—he seems to want . . .
HENRY. I can guess what he wants! (*The Stranger puts his right hand out, swings it across his chest towards the hut.*)
SUSAN. Oh, I don't think so.
HENRY. The cad. Wait till I get my hands on him.
SUSAN. He's awfully strong. (*She moves downstage of Stranger. Stranger bows.*)
HENRY. He may be—I'll fix him when I'm free again.
SUSAN. And awfully sweet really.
HENRY. Sweet! Sweet the way he ties us up, wasn't it? Philip, I think you might say something.
PHILIP. Say what? I'm considering. (*The Stranger kneels.*)
SUSAN. Don't worry, dear, I'm sure he doesn't mean to upset me.

(*The Stranger bows with his head to the ground.*) Oh, he's got lovely manners.
HENRY. There must be some way out.
SUSAN. All right, but what?
HENRY. Susan, you must fly.
SUSAN. Fly? Without my shoes? (*Gives her hands to Stranger.*) He'd catch me at once and then he might take his revenge on you. He's got an enormous knife, don't forget.
HENRY. Has he now? You might use it like Judith.
SUSAN. Horrid idea. (*The Stranger bows, his hands against his shoulders.*) What is it, Your Royal Highness? (*The Stranger bows, Susan backing up to hut during the next lines.*)
PHILIP. There. He's off again.
HENRY. Philip, are you thinking?
PHILIP. No, my mind is a blank.
SUSAN. (*Just below hut.*) I must say this Prince is rather obstinate. Just one moment, sir, and I am yours. (*Crosses to Henry and Philip at mast.*) Listen, I have an idea His Royal Highness won't untie you unless . . . until . . .
HENRY. That's it . . .
PHILIP. Well, ask him his terms, dear. (*Susan goes towards The Stranger and asks him by signs.*)
HENRY. Philip!
PHILIP. No histrionics. We may as well know the terms of our release. Find out from him, Susan.
HENRY. You won't accept?
PHILIP. I have no alternative, unfortunately.
HENRY. My God, man, act—do something.
PHILIP. Act yourself, old fellow.
HENRY. I shall never be able to feel the same towards you after this, Philip, never.
PHILIP. Towards *me*—well, I must say. . . . (*Susan has asked the question, and received a bow from The Stranger in reply: she moves across stage below Philip and Henry to mast.*)
SUSAN. (*Delighted.*) All right, darling, it's yes.
PHILIP. Yes what?
SUSAN. His Royal Highness will let you both go as soon . . .
HENRY. As soon as what?
SUSAN. Oh, Henry, what a bore you are! It's not so easy con-

versing in signs with a Crown Prince. I don't know exactly, dear, as soon . . .

HENRY. Well, I do know exactly. Tell the Crown Prince, by signs, that I'd like a word with him.

SUSAN. That wouldn't be the slightest good. You two are poles apart.

HENRY. Poles apart, Philip. It's quite clear she thinks this ravaging savage is superior to me.

SUSAN. Oh, no, now, darlings, what shall I do? I can't leave you tied up there for days and days, perhaps to be eaten up by ants, can I? Well, dear, can I? (*To Philip.*) See you presently, darling. (*Goes to Stranger.*) After you, Your Highness. (*The Stranger goes into the hut. Susan gives look towards the mast and follows him in. Pause.*)

HENRY. And tomorrow morning she'll say she saw a geranium or a tulip in the sky, and that means . . . (*Silence.*) Philip, so a chap has come along, just as I wished. Don't tell me you feel quite happy about this?

PHILIP. (*Not listening, his eye on the doorway of the hut.*) Why are they waiting?

HENRY. What for?

PHILIP. The curtain.

HENRY. That's good. You don't imagine His Royal Highness is going to bother about a curtain, do you?

HENRY *and* PHILIP. Curtain! (*An invisible hand releases the curtain which falls over the doorway. The stage curtain is coming down as Philip says:*)

PHILIP. Ah! There it is at last!

CURTAIN

ACT III

The following morning.
Philip is sitting R. *of the table on a faded and renovated deck chair. Susan is sitting on another one upstage of the table. In the middle of the table is the remains of a large and beautiful fish. Henry is halfway up the mast sitting on he cross bar looking out to sea through a telescope. Philip and Susan are eating with homemade forks.*

SUSAN. Stupid you are not to have some fish. It's heaven. The sauce! I can't make sauce like that.
PHILIP. Oh, yes, you can, dear, it's just the cinnamon.
HENRY. Hope it chokes you.
SUSAN. You are a grumpy old thing. However, if you want to go on a hunger strike, do—it will make cooking much easier, only two to feed.
HENRY. I'm not on a hunger strike at all. I refuse to touch that fish—very naturally, you'd think.
PHILIP. There's nothing else for luncheon, you know.
HENRY. Then I go luncheonless.
SUSAN. Naughty and silly. (*Holds up fish's head.*) He really has a sweet face.
HENRY. Who has a sweet face?
SUSAN. The fish.
HENRY. This friend of yours, is he supplying all our food from now on? I suppose it comes from the royal cuisine of his father the King? By special appointment?
SUSAN. Well, speaking as a gourmet, I only hope he will.
PHILIP. Yes, and with all respect to darling Mrs. B., I hope so too. Come on, Henry, have a taste.
HENRY. I wonder you don't send Susan off to live with him in his royal hut, on condition that he brings you fried fish and chips twice a day. He'd be happy, Susan would be happy and you'd be

happy, and I know how much you like happiness. (*Swings down from mast.*)

SUSAN. There. He's off again.

HENRY. In heaven's name, where is your self-respect?

SUSAN. Meaning exactly?

HENRY. I can't get over your attitude. When this beast in human form springs on us out of his jungle, half kills Philip and me, ties us up and leads you to a fate worse than death you put on the most affected act I ever saw, simper, bob up and down, call him Sir, and let him stroll away as if nothing had happened.

SUSAN. Just tell me how I could have stopped him?

HENRY. Perhaps you couldn't have stopped him, but at least you didn't have to go on making low curtsies long after he was out of sight. Let that pass, we all know what a little snob you are. The one I can't forgive is Philip.

PHILIP. Me? (*Turns to Henry.*)

HENRY. Yes, you. When Tarzan of the Apes came back this morning with a piece of fish, did you thrash him? You did not. You tucked into that fish as if you had never seen food before. It's absolutely horrible. He's only got to come back with the pudding to be your friend for life. Then between coconut time and dinner I suppose he'll tie Philip and me up again or send us fishing.

PHILIP. (*Rises and crosses to leaf.*) May I point out that neither did you thrash him? Very sensible, considering his physique and that he was stripped for action. Nor did you tell him what you thought of him. Not that it'd have been much good, unless done by signs. (*Lying down.*)

SUSAN. (*Picks up bag and fan.*) And may I ask what you mean by a fate worse than death? I'd like to remind you that we fixed a tariff with this Prince. No need to call him names—he was perfectly correct in his behavior.

HENRY. Oh, I know to you a Crown Prince couldn't be incorrect. The soul of chivalry, no doubt.

SUSAN. I'm glad you realize it.

HENRY. Of course. (*Rises.*)

SUSAN. (*Rises.*) He is a noble savage and a great, great dear. (*Goes into hut for finger bowl and towel, leaves bag and fan in hut.*)

HENRY. Philip, you just heard what she said. Now do you think his behavior was correct?

PHILIP. (*Sitting up.*) Incorrect. Improper. Dishonest. Objectionable. Unreasonable. Immoral. Criminal, Fishy.
HENRY. Well, I'm glad you agree with me.
PHILIP. Wrong, not right. Perfectly out of order, by our standards.
HENRY. By any standards.
PHILIP. No, Henry. It isn't everybody who's ruled by modern English ethics—look at the People of the Veil. (*Susan enters with finger bowl and towel and goes upstage of Philip. Henry sits on yellow stool.*) Here on this island we are living under primitive conditions. (*To Susan.*) Oh, thank you, dear. This Prince has a large tribe, no doubt, at his beck and call, each member of it more savage than himself—would it not be foolish to make a desperate enemy of him? We must placate him. (*Gives towel back to Susan.*)
HENRY. Appeasement.
PHILIP. Precisely.
HENRY. Well, I don't care for it and I intend to resist.
PHILIP. How?
HENRY. Morally, by passive resistance. I shall go into the underground movement. (*Rises.*) I shall not touch his stinking fish.
SUSAN. You do keep on about the fish. (*Into hut with finger bowl and towel.*)
HENRY. It's symbolic. This man is stronger than I am, no good using force. Very well then, I express myself by means of fasting.
PHILIP. And then?
HENRY. I come to no terms with an enemy I despise.
SUSAN. (*Re-entering from hut.*) If you go on teasing him, he may kill you.
HENRY. Let him.
SUSAN. But think how stupid you'd feel if he killed you and the next day a ship arrived.
HENRY. (*Rises.*) All right. Eat his fish until you burst. (*Stranger, with head dress and small lei, enters from behind hut carrying a dish of fruit.*) And go into the hut with him whenever he feels like it—I couldn't care less. Here comes Mr. X. with the pudding. What did I say?
SUSAN. Oh, sir, how lovely. Thank you and Your Royal Highness. (*Points to fish.*) The fish—a dream. (*Makes signs of appreciation. Stranger offers dish to Philip who bows, points to fish and*

claps his hands. Stranger gives him fruit dish, then lifts fish off table and hands it to Henry.)
HENRY. Matey, aren't you? Then of course you would be.
SUSAN. Henry! Henry! (*Sits in chair.*) You must stop . . .
HENRY. How Philip can sit there while you flap your pretty little eyelids up and down, listening to the rivers of rubbish which pour out of that pretty little mouth . . . (*Stranger has given fish to Henry, now picks up leaf from top of table and puts it behind the hut.*)
SUSAN. Don't take any notice, darling, he's hungry and fractious, poor him. (*To Stranger as he comes downstage.*) Oh, sir, why can't you speak to us? You'll never know how much I long for the recipe of that heavenly sauce.
STRANGER. I give it you. (*Takes table to upstage of hut. Susan looks at Henry and then at Stranger.*)
HENRY. (*As he crosses.*) Philip! He spoke English. Who are you?
STRANGER. I'm Danish, from Copenhagen, shipwrecked like you.
SUSAN. Oh, no!
STRANGER. Ship's cook. (*Takes fish from Henry and moves off behind hut* U. L. *Susan cries. They are dumbstruck. Philip sits in chair. Henry starts the Stranger's dance and dances to Susan's* L.)
HENRY. Poor old Susan. His Royal Highness, the cook. (*Barks at Susan.*) Oh, sir, what's for dinner today? (*Susan starts to cry.*) Of course, cookery is a princely science . . .
PHILIP. Oh, do be quiet a minute . . .
HENRY. But let's hope he won't call up his tribe, a tribe of cooks, each one more savage than himself, and spoil our broth, oh, I do hope not. Shouldn't think so, as we've been so terribly nice to him, eh, Philip?
PHILIP. Henry, if you could control yourself and give us a moment to think about this . . .
SUSAN. (*Furiously.*) What are you two men waiting for?
HENRY. The coffee, I suppose, and Imperial Tokay. Coffee, Philip? (*Claps his hands. Moves to hut, leans on it.*)
SUSAN. You're two to one now, aren't you? He's just a lonely cook, he hasn't got a regiment of head-hunters or anything! Go on, beat him up!
HENRY. Why beat him up, all of a sudden?
SUSAN. Don't you realize he's not a Prince at all, he's made utter dupes of us, passing himself off as royalty, making me curtsy . . .

HENRY. (*Between Susan and Philip.*) If it was only curtsying, dear!
PHILIP. Henry!
SUSAN. I don't know what young people are coming to. It's just as the magistrates always say, the moment they get out of reform school they go straight to the movies and all the good is undone again. A real savage would never have behaved like that—he'd have been afraid of the totem. I've yet to find the cook who's afraid of anything. It's the mistress who's always terrified. But this time I'm not terrified, I'm far too angry, and so ought you to be. (*To Henry.*) If you had any guts at all you'd beat him up now.
PHILIP. (*Rises.*) Darling, how can we—he isn't here.
SUSAN. Well, tally-ho! After him—surround him.
HENRY. Tally-ho! (*Dancing round mast.*) Tally-ho, tally-ho, Philip, Henry! Wait, Philip, I'll come round.
PHILIP. Henry—Henry, this is no time for square dancing. Don't be silly, dear, two of us can't surround him.
SUSAN. (*Rises.*) You're not going to take any revenge? You don't mind what he's done?
PHILIP. Yes, I do. I'm very annoyed with him.
HENRY. And I, on the contrary (*Gets fruit.*) feel quite differently about the whole affair.
SUSAN. Oh, do you? (*Fanning.*)
HENRY. (*Sits in chair.*) Well, of course. Yesterday we had a great tribe of Red Indians, or whatever it is, breathing down our necks . . . (*Pulls fruit round in front of him.*)
SUSAN. No, we hadn't.
HENRY. We thought we had—comes to the same thing. Today it's just coping with the kitchen staff. Susan can sack him.
SUSAN. Oh, Henry!
PHILIP. Really, Henry, you're not being very constructive.
SUSAN. He's got to be punished.
HENRY. What for? Being a cook?
SUSAN. (*To Philip.*) Darling, you're on my side, aren't you?
PHILIP. Yes, darling, of course I am. But we have to remember that he's stronger than we are, much younger, and armed with a great kitchen knife, which he obviously knows how to use.
SUSAN. We must tie him up, that's all—tie him to the mast then he won't be able to use it.
PHILIP. Tie him to the mast?

SUSAN. Yes, it's his turn, isn't it? (*Goes to mast, gets rope from it, goes to Philip and puts it on his knee.*)
PHILIP. Well, I'm bound to say it is, but first catch your hare.
HENRY. Or in this case your heir apparent! (*Laughs.*)
SUSAN. Henry! I've had quite enough. (*Susan slaps his face, picks up the fruit and takes it into the hut, coming out again immediately.*)
HENRY. She struck me!
PHILIP. Serves you right, Henry. Here we are in a very puzzling situation, and you sit there making schoolboy jokes.
HENRY. What a spiteful thing to say! What's puzzling, old boy?
PHILIP. Perfectly obvious. We've got to deal with this young man somehow or other, we can't let things go on like this.
HENRY. I thought you were so pleased, enjoying your luncheon and so on.
PHILIP. We must find out who he is.
HENRY. He's told you—he's a Danish cook.
PHILIP. That's what he said just now—yesterday he said he was a Prince of the islands, and tomorrow he may say he's Errol Flynn. It isn't good enough. I would like to cross-examine him, and I think Susan's idea of tying him up is a very good one. The question is how?
SUSAN. Listen, I've got an idea. We must use cunning as he did. It's time for our siesta. Now, you two lie down and pretend to be asleep. I'll get him up against the mast somehow or other, then you fling yourselves upon him—Henry, you lasso him round the neck while Philip ties him up. Simple?
PHILIP. That ought to work all right.
HENRY. If you ask me, we're going to make ghastly fools of ourselves for nothing. (*Philip lies down near his chair.*)
SUSAN. It won't be the first time, darling, will it? Now, lie down. I'll go and find him. (*Pulls Henry up.*) Don't move till you hear me say Psst! (*Looks back at Henry, still standing.*) Henry darling, you know how to lie down. (*Exits calling.*) Hillooo!
HENRY. You know, Philip, we shouldn't pander to her.
PHILIP. We're not pandering to her, we're just protecting ourselves.
HENRY. We must look like two assassinated French Presidents.
PHILIP. Why must we?

HENRY. Haven't you noticed they're always assassinated in evening dress?
PHILIP. Surely not two at a time. (*Susan crosses stage behind hut calling "Hillooo!" Exits.*) Now, don't bungle your act, Henry.
HENRY. (*Taking rope and tying knot.*) Haven't lassoed anybody for years. Have you?
PHILIP. You want a slip knot.
HENRY. Yes, I know that.
PHILIP. Now lie down and close your eyes.
HENRY. Shall I snore?
PHILIP. Why?
HENRY. Make it more lifelike.
PHILIP. I thought you never snored.
HENRY. I do when I've got a cold.
PHILIP. But you haven't got a cold. Now lie down and keep quiet.
SUSAN. Hilloo! (*Enters.*)
HENRY. (*Sits up and moves nearer to Philip.*) She's got him, Philip, she's got him, old boy.
SUSAN. Psst! Henry! (*Henry lies down, left knee raised, the rope lying on his chest. The Stranger enters and sees them. Pointing to them.*) Asleep!
STRANGER. Wonderful. (*Picks Susan up and moves towards the hut. Susan shakes her head and signs to him to put her down. He does so. She signs to Henry and Philip, herself and the hut, signifying that she cannot go into the hut whilst they are there. The Stranger nods understanding, looks at them, then picks up the nearest chair and hands it to her, as she is pointing towards the mast. She looks at it, takes it and puts it upstage of cactus. He then moves to between Henry and Philip, kneels, takes the rope which he slips under Henry's knee, then he tickles the sole of Philip's right foot. Susan, amazed, goes to mast, and hiding what she is doing from The Stranger, gets rope ready. Philip raises his right foot, moves it slightly and drops it again. The Stranger tickles it again, and this time Philip lifts it and drops it across Henry's left foot. The Stranger quickly ties them together. He rises and looks towards Susan, who beckons him toward her. He goes, putting one hand each side of the mast. Susan slips the noose round his hands, pulls it tight, and runs round the mast until he is well tied up, taking the rope round his neck once on the third round.*)
STRANGER. (*As she tightens the noose.*) *Vacht fannen air day.*

Vacht layver du! (Philip and Henry try to spring to their feet but fall back as they are tied together. During the following lines they get themselves untied, and Susan ties the Stranger to the mast.)
PHILIP. Help, help! They've got me! They've got me. Henry, what are you doing? Untie me at once.
STRANGER. *Satans kayling—vorfor binner my.*
HENRY. I am untying you.
PHILIP. Well, pull then.
HENRY. I am pulling.
PHILIP. Well, push.
HENRY. I am pushing.
PHILIP. Well, let's get together.
HENRY. We are together, that's just the point.
SUSAN. Do stop quarrelling, you idiots!
HENRY. Philip, look, look, she's done it.
PHILIP. (*Seeing that Susan has tied The Stranger to the mast herself, rises, and goes to her.*) Really, dear, you should have waited for us. You might have strained yourself.
HENRY. (*Sitting cross-legged, facing mast.*) It was rather wonderful.
PHILIP. Is it quite secure? Better have his knife. (*Takes knife.*) Sit down, dear, you must be tired. (*Susan sits on chair.*) Sit down, Henry, oh, you are sitting down. (*To Stranger.*) You can stand. Now, let's get to the bottom of this. You say you were the ship's cook?
STRANGER. Cook.
PHILIP. On our ship?
STRANGER. Yes.
HENRY. Yes, well, I don't remember you.
STRANGER. Don't remember you either. We were never actually introduced.
PHILIP. This is a statement we can verify. If you were the ship's cook, perhaps you can tell us what we had for dinner the night of the wreck?
STRANGER. Night of the wreck?
HENRY. You've got him there!
STRANGER. Yes. I am giving consomme madrilene, or Bisque doumar . . .
PHILIP. I had the Bisque, I remember.

STRANGER. A Sole Veronique, a choice of Tournedos Rossini, or Poulet a L'Estragon. A nice Camembert and fruits *rafraîchies.*
HENRY. Well, I never got any fruits *rafraîchies.*
PHILIP. That's the fault of that wretched steward, he never looked after our table properly. Thank God we never tipped him.
SUSAN. I think he's proved his point, don't you?
PHILIP. Well, now where have you been since the wreck?
STRANGER. Two Danish miles from here is a small cove where I am building my house.
HENRY. (*Lies down.*) And when are you becoming aware of our presence, pray?
STRANGER. About a week ago.
PHILIP. That was during your week on.
STRANGER. Week on?
PHILIP. Never you mind. Now, what made you dress up like that?
STRANGER. In my country we have a saying, "*Man mor hooler son de ulver air iblandt.*" It means, one must howl like the wolves one is amongst.
SUSAN. What does that mean?
HENRY. When in Rome do as Romans do.
PHILIP. I never heard such nonsense. None of us are dressed up in that affected manner.
STRANGER. What else could I wear? I do not possess the Tuxedo.
PHILIP. Tuxedo?
HENRY. He means he hasn't got a dinner jacket.
PHILIP. Oh, poor chap. We can't get him one here. Now, when you first met my wife . . .
STRANGER. Your wife! The lady is your wife? I have made a big mistake.
HENRY. (*Rises.*) Oh, so you thought she was my wife?
PHILIP. No, no, Henry.
HENRY. That makes it even more serious.
STRANGER. No, no, you misunderstand me. I did not think the lady could have been married to either. That would have made a big difference.
HENRY. Why?
STRANGER. *Min dedste vens kone har jeg kun broderlige fleuser* or as we say in Denmark that means for the wife of my friend I am a brother!
PHILIP. Oh, no. We don't want to start all that again.

SUSAN. The point is what are we going to do with him?
PHILIP. We can't leave him tied up there for ever, you know.
HENRY. I don't see why not.
PHILIP. We'd have to keep bringing him bread and water.
HENRY. I don't mind watering him now and again.
PHILIP. What about exercise?
SUSAN. I don't mind taking him for walks. (*Henry looks at Susan, smacks his hand.*)
PHILIP. Now, supposing—I don't say we will—but supposing we set you free without any further punishment, what would you do?
HENRY. Would you go back to your house and stay there?
STRANGER. (*Pathetically.*) It's awfully lonely there.
PHILIP. (*Hard-hearted.*) Yes, I daresay it is.
STRANGER. No soul to speak with all day. I might get sick, no one would ever know.
HENRY. If you get sick, send for me.
STRANGER. (*With a threatening look.*) I might go mad all by myself . . . could not be responsible . . . might go berserk.
PHILIP. I don't think I should care to have this fellow skulking about in the undergrowth, peering at us from behind trees, going mad and so on. I don't think I should have an easy moment . . . (*Looks at Susan.*)
HENRY. Well, he can't stay here with us, can he?
PHILIP. Why not?
HENRY. You don't expect me to sit down at the same table as the ship's cook, do you?
PHILIP. It's certainly not an ideal arrangement.
HENRY. And another thing. Do you expect Susan to provide his meals as well as ours? Why should she slave her fingers to the bone . . .
SUSAN. (*Rises and crosses to* R. *of Henry, facing Philip.*) Listen, I've thought it all out. He's a cook, isn't he? And a very good cook, too. Let's make him our cook.
PHILIP. That's an idea.
HENRY. I think it's the most immoral suggestion I've ever heard.
PHILIP. What nonsense, Henry. It's simply a question of whether he cooks for us, or we cook for him. I vote he cooks for us. (*Holds up hand.*)
SUSAN. So do I. (*Holds hand up.*)
PHILIP. The "I's" have it.

SUSAN. Well, then, is it all settled?
PHILIP. Yes. Henry can do the washing up.
SUSAN. Good. Now, you listen to me. Things have changed since yesterday. You're tied up now, and I'm giving orders, and my orders are that from now on you'll do all the cooking. We have a continental breakfast, then we usually lunch about one-thirty . . .
PHILIP. Just three things, soup, fish or an egg dish, and sweet or pudding, fruit of course.
SUSAN. (*Starts to untie Stranger, passing the rope to Philip each time.*) We none of us bother about tea, so you can have the afternoons off.
PHILIP. You'll do the hut work, valet Mr. Henry and myself. Do you agree?
STRANGER. (*Now untied.*) O.K.
PHILIP. And in future I shall expect you to give my wife every satisfaction.
HENRY. Philip! (*Susan looks at him puzzled. Henry slaps his leg.*)
PHILIP. I could have phrased that better. You'll call my wife Madam. What's your name?
STRANGER. Philip.
PHILIP. We don't want any more familiarity. What's your name?
STRANGER. My name is Philip.
PHILIP. Is it? That's very awkward. I shall call you Stanley.
SUSAN. Why Stanley?
PHILIP. It's a good jungle name, dear.
SUSAN. Now, darlings, leave us alone for a few minutes, will you? (*Stranger moves up to hut, and brings Henry's and Philip's hats to them.*)
PHILIP. Why?
HENRY. Why?
SUSAN. I want a word with him, that's all.
PHILIP. What, you and cook, dear? I don't think I quite care for that. (*Henry rises. Stranger hands them their hats.*) Well, he's got the hat checks right, anyway. (*Susan kisses Philip.*)
SUSAN. Run along, dear, please, just for three minutes. (*Stranger goes back to hut. As Philip and Henry move upstage he holds out their fishing rods, they move off. He replaces the fishing rods against hut wall.*)
PHILIP. (*As they go.*) Two minutes.
SUSAN. I really must give you a little talking to, you know. First

of all, I didn't want to mention it in front of my . . . colleagues, but must ask you not to smile every time you look at me. You think it's a joke, but it's no joke at all to be shipwrecked, it's a very sad situation for a woman. (*Pauses and looks at Stranger.*) Why are you smiling now? What can have come over you yesterday? I always thought Danes were good, but you behaved like a savage. I suppose you're descended from Vikings, yes, that must be it. You must have had a kind of Viking dream, and now you've woken up, and so I'll forget everything until the moment you came in with that heavenly fish, and you can call me Madam, and the work won't be much. I'm sorry we had to tie you up, but it's all over now, and we trust you completely. I shall call you Joe, I think . . . . (*Stranger kneels and kisses her hand.*) Stanley is too stupid! (*Under yesterday's spell.*) Oh, Your Royal Highness! (*Remembering.*) Oh, Joe, off with you, off to the kitchen. Oh, I've just remembered something.

STRANGER. What ees it?

SUSAN. When I first saw you, I presented my husband to you. Oh, Joe, you knew I was married all the time, aren't you ashamed of yourself? (*The Stranger bows in the old way, and exits. Scratching her arms.*) Oh, well, no use crying over spilt milk! (*Dances off. Enter Philip and Henry.*)

HENRY. I don't like it, Philip.

PHILIP. Nonsense, Henry. Dottie runs her whole house with problem boys. They don't mind what they do.

HENRY. It's an entirely different situation with Dottie. Weren't we meeting them here? (*Henry notices that the stage is empty. Runs to hut doorway and looks inside. Turns to Philip, shakes his head.*)

PHILIP. You know, you'll never keep a cook if you don't trust him.

HENRY. Well, where is "Jungle Jim"? (*Hangs his hat on hut. Philip claps his hands and The Stranger enters carrying a leaf tray with coffee pot and two cups. He crosses to Philip and hands them to him, then goes upstage for table.*)

PHILIP. Oh, there you are. (*Taking coffee tray.*) Oh, thank you. Isn't that nice, Henry, the set must be for export only.

HENRY. What's that?

PHILIP. Coffee, of course.

STRANGER. (*Putting table in place on Philip's* L., *takes tray from*

Philip, puts it on table.) I am sorry it is late, the meal was a little interrupted.

PHILIP. That's all right, you'll take a day to settle down, I expect. *(The Stranger goes to side of hut, gets umbrella, opens it, and sticks it in the ground* R. *of Philip. After setting the umbrella, Stranger gets large shell which he brings to Philip to act as a footstool.)* I think we're going to be very comfortable here. We've obviously found a treasure. *(Pouring out coffee, Philip tries to drink coffee, the strands of his hat get in the way. Stranger lifts loose ends of hat as Philip lifts cup to mouth.)* Where's your mistress?

HENRY. Philip!

PHILIP. Where's Madam?

STRANGER. Gone shopping. *(Philip takes hat off and hands it to Stranger.)*

PHILIP. Well, what are we waiting for?

STRANGER. Please, can I have my knife? *(Henry goes upstage for rope, brings it to below mast, and starts to tie a slip knot.)*

PHILIP. Why do you want your knife?

STRANGER. Please, to cook the dinner.

PHILIP. That's quite reasonable. *(Gives him the knife.)* There you are. Thank you.

STRANGER. Thank you. *(Exits, throwing Philip's hat under large leaf as he goes.)*

HENRY. And don't go cutting yourself. *(Winds rope up.)*

PHILIP. I must say that's a weight off my mind. I was so worried last night I hardly slept. I couldn't quite see how it was going to end. Trust clever little Susan to turn the whole thing to our advantage, bless her.

HENRY. Bless her indeed.

PHILIP. You must admit it was a stroke of genius transforming a dangerous savage into a Danish cook. You said yourself we could do with an orderly here. Aren't you pleased now?

HENRY. Oddly enough, no.

PHILIP. Ah! You've brought a grievance back from your walk, I see.

HENRY. Exactly. *(Throws rope into hut.)* I've thought it all over. Now I begin to see everything crystal clear.

PHILIP. I am always a little alarmed when you begin to see things crystal clear.

HENRY. Because you go through life in blinkers.

PHILIP. Quite happy as I am.
HENRY. (*Pauses, then turns to Philip.*) Exactly, a cloud has passed—a subject is closed—nothing shocks you.
PHILIP. I wouldn't say that, Henry, I was shocked at the time, very shocked.
HENRY. But I wonder if you happened to notice that Susan was never shocked—not the least little bit—until she discovered that the cook was a cook? Did that strike you at all?
PHILIP. Logical, in my view. She did what she had to do to save us in a perfectly cheerful and dignified way. Discovering that she has been the victim of a hoax, she is, very naturally, in a rage. I don't blame her, and I don't see why you should.
HENRY. That's right, twist it round to suit yourself. You've always been as blind as a bat where Susan is concerned and I suppose you always will be.
PHILIP. Hold your horses, old boy.
HENRY. No—the time has come for a little plain speaking. (*Philip puts cup on tray, saucer on cup.*) Blind as a bat. For six years I had an affair with Susan under your very nose and you never suspected a thing. Six years, Philip.
PHILIP. I don't understand the object of this outburst, and I'm beginning to find it a bore.
HENRY. Home truths often are a bore, but I feel it's my duty to speak out.
PHILIP. According to you, Susan was only annoyed when the man turned out to be a cook. Are you implying that until then she thoroughly enjoyed the whole thing?
HENRY. You've said it. I wouldn't have put it quite so broadly.
PHILIP. That's very good of you.
HENRY. She seemed to be rather unnaturally—shall we say—resigned. She hardly demurred—she just skipped into the hut.
PHILIP. She did it to save us.
HENRY. Yes, but so quickly. It upset me very much and, if you ask me, old man, it's not the first time she's done it.
PHILIP. Done what?
HENRY. Been unfaithful to us.
PHILIP. How dare you talk like that, Henry!
HENRY. I've begun to realize that if you've been blind, so have I. Here's a girl with two good husbands, honest, decent men, when like as not, she's been playing fast and loose with us both for years.

PHILIP. I'd put my hand in the fire that Susan's never been unfaithful to me.
HENRY. Poor old boy.
PHILIP. I know what I know. Susan has never been unfaithful to me.
HENRY. Then how about me?
PHILIP. You? Oh, I don't count you.
HENRY. What d'you mean, don't count me?
PHILIP. I don't count you—I don't know why but I don't count you.
HENRY. So that's why you were able to sleep so peacefully in the little hut?
PHILIP. And now every word you've been saying, every insulting implication, has clearly shown me you don't love Susan one little bit.
HENRY. Oh, so I don't love Susan, don't I?
PHILIP. If you did you'd never bring such unfair charges against her.
HENRY. Can't you see it's because I love her? I'm out of my mind with jealousy—I can't help noticing every little detail of her behavior and brooding over it—that's jealousy, old boy, that's love. You're the one that doesn't love her, and doesn't know what it is to be jealous.
PHILIP. Oh, yes, I do. I felt jealous when you first told me about you and Susan.
HENRY. (*Picks up green footstool.*) All I can say is you showed remarkable self-control, disserting on logic and the polygamy of women. Then what about yesterday? When we were trussed up to that maypole you weren't jealous at all—you never raised a finger. (*Puts footstool below chair.*)
PHILIP. But what could I have done?
HENRY. (*Sits in chair, feet on green stool.*) You could have registered a protest, if nothing else.
PHILIP. You were registering enough for both of us. Never heard such a noise as you made.
HENRY. It would have been more human to join in. Then look at the way you ate that fish.
PHILIP. Oh, my God—we're not back to that fish again, are we?
HENRY. That fish is the symbol of your attitude. You pretend to

love Susan, yet you can eat that fish. To me, to me that fish represented Susan in the arms of . . .

PHILIP. (*Rises.*) Really, Henry, you've gone too far. I thought you were supposed to be our friend.

HENRY. (*Stricken, rises.*) Philip. I'm sorry, old chap.

PHILIP. Well, yes, I should hope so. Don't know what's the matter with you.

HENRY. It's this bloody island—I need a holiday, old boy.

PHILIP. Henry, don't always look on the gloomy side of everything; it makes you so depressing.

HENRY. Yes. I beg your pardon—I'm sorry.

PHILIP. (*Pats his shoulder.*) All right. Now cheer up. Everybody's remarking about it, old boy.

HENRY. It sounds rather silly, I suppose, but our friendship means a great deal to me, Philip.

PHILIP. Yes, of course. It means a great deal to me too.

HENRY. Now, Philip, I have news for you.

PHILIP. News?

HENRY. Good news. I've made a decision and I want you to be the first to hear about it. I've decided once and for all to finish with Susan.

PHILIP. (*Horrified.*) My dear old Henry, do try and calm down. Think what it would be like if when we got home you found you'd quarrelled with Susan—we should all be simply wretched . . . (*Pushes Henry down onto stool.*)

HENRY. It's the only way . . .

PHILIP. No, no, it's quite impossible—you love us and we love you. Sit down. I only said you didn't love Susan just now because I lost my temper, but of course I know you do, you adore her. Like me, you couldn't get on without her. You keep asking me what I thought about in the little hut—very well, I'll tell you. I imagined that, instead of being safe here with us, Susan had been drowned and that you and I were living alone, each in his hut. You say I never mind what happens, but I can tell you that would have finished me off. Nothing to look forward to, nothing to work for, no more fun and no more happiness. A vivid picture came to me of Susan in her evening dress, floating about on the moonlit water, and for ages I couldn't get it out of my mind. Then I remembered that here we all are safe and sound, that Susan was a few yards away, with you, and that next morning I should see her darling little face and have her to talk and laugh with all day and every day—well, then, my dear old Henry, I realized my luck and went happily off to sleep again. And snored. Now do you see? (*They look at each other with affection. Henry takes out his handkerchief and wipes his eyes, then Philip takes his out. They blow their noses —together, "Hoot, hoot." As they do so a siren goes. They repeat this once more. Again the siren "Hoot, hoot." The third time Henry blows his nose but not Philip. "Hoot, hoot." They realize it is a ship.*)

HENRY. A ship! Philip, a ship! (*Slapping Philip's knee.*)

PHILIP. Keep calm, keep absolutely calm.

HENRY. It's a ship!

PHILIP. All right, don't frighten it away.

HENRY. Susan—Susan ——!

PHILIP. All right, I'll fire the rocket. (*Gets them from the hut window.*) Here are the sticks.

HENRY. (*Taking sticks from him.*) No, no, let me.

PHILIP. No, please let me, Henry.

HENRY. No, no, youngest unmarried man.

PHILIP. But it's my invention—it might explode.

HENRY. That's what it's meant to do, isn't it?

PHILIP. Yes, I suppose it is.

HENRY. (*Rubs the two sticks together, they burst into flame, applies stick to back of mast.*) Baden Powell was right. (*There is an explosion, the flash coming out of the gramophone horn. The explosion makes the coconuts droop to their lowest mark and slowly ascends as music plays and the gramophone starts to play the samba. The Stranger enters.*)

PHILIP. Coco-powder, an entirely new explosive. I'm a munitions king. Henry, you stay there, I'll go down to the beach and meet them.

HENRY. Right! (*Philip exits behind hut, The Stranger picks up the umbrella and holding it over Philip's head, exits with him. Henry looks off through the telescope. Susan enters from below hut.*)

SUSAN. (*To Henry, who comes down the mast.*) A perfectly enormous ship. They've seen me. They ran up a signal—England Expects, I expect. I signalled back with my stole. They've lowered a boat. Where's Philip?

HENRY. Gone down to meet them. Susan, when we get home everything must be like the old days again.
SUSAN. Yes, yes, darling, of course it will be.
HENRY. No, wait, it was a terrible mistake ever telling Philip.
SUSAN. What did I say?
HENRY. And now we must pretend—we must pretend that all is over between us.
SUSAN. I see, back to the old days again.
HENRY. Then we can take up where we left off, and everything will be all right.
SUSAN. Paradise, yes. Clever Henry.
HENRY. So you agree, that all is over between us.
SUSAN. Absolutely, blissfully over. (*Hugs him. Philip enters.*)
PHILIP. What's all over, dear? They're lowering a boat.
SUSAN. (*Turning quickly, and hugging him.*) Our absolutely blissful holiday on this absolutely blissful island.
PHILIP. Yes, I must say I've enjoyed every moment of it. We must certainly come again. (*Susan goes into hut.*) Now, we must start packing. It's an enormous ship, Henry, another cruise, I think.
HENRY. Perhaps our tickets are still good. (*Exits to hut.*)
PHILIP. (*Gets hat from under leaf.*) Have you seen my butterfly net anywhere? I thought I had it here somewhere. (*A monkey leaps on from above tree and hands him the net.*) Oh, thanks, Henry, old boy, you always know where everything is. (*Goes into hut. The monkey leaps onto the crossbar of the mast, then turns, still on the bar, to face* L. *Susan comes out of the hut and sees him. Calls:*)
SUSAN. Oh, Philip . . . Henry . . . look! A monkey on a stick! (*Philip and Henry come out of the hut, Philip to her* R. *and Henry on her* L.) Oh, what luck. That means seven years of utter bliss! (*The monkey drops off the mast onto the mound and looks at them. They move closer to him.*) Oh, what a pretty monkey. Can't we take him home with us, Philip? (*The monkey bows as The Stranger did in Act II.*)
PHILIP. Certainly not, dear, we've got Stanley. (*Siren till curtain falls. They all three rush off below hut. The monkey makes a gesture of annoyance, then sits sadly at the foot of the mast as*)

THE CURTAIN FALLS

PROPERTY PLOT

Rope clothesline attached to mast
Umbrella
Large shell
Shell bag for Susan with powder, lipstick, clothes brush
Hammock between mast and tree
Phonograph on mast, cord hanging down
Nuts on tree—to be shaken down
Butterfly net
Basket of butterflies
Cork with butterflies
In hut: 3 half coconuts on leaf tray, rockets, sticks, turban, broom, palm leaves, finger bowl, towel
Flowers
Fishing tackle
3 round fruits
Shaving kit—razor, soap, talc
Laundry basket with clean shirt for Philip and 2 clothes pegs
Palm leaves
Needle and thread
Fruit and leaves over bamboo stick
2 nuts on sticks with faces painted on them
Straw shoes
Straw cravat
Bow and arrow
Feathered headdress
Lei of flowers—2
Handkerchiefs for Philip and Henry
2 deck chairs
Table
Fish
Telescope
Forks (homemade)
Fan
Dish of fruit
Knife—Stranger
Leaf tray
Coffee pot, 2 cups